The
Full-Plate Detox

The Time-Starved SHEro's Guide for Getting Back to the Top of Her Priority List Guilt Free!

NICOLE CHAMBLIN

The
Full-Plate Detox

The Time-Starved SHEro's Guide for Getting
Back to the Top of Her Priority List Guilt Free!

NICOLE CHAMBLIN

Copyright © 2020 by Nicole Chamblin
Published by Truth2RenewHearts Publishing
An imprint of Truth2RenewHearts Enterprises, LLC
Pittsburgh, Pennsylvania

For information:
www.Truth2RenewHeartsPublishing.com
info@Truth2RenewHeartsPublishing.com

ISBN: 978-1-7345646-0-0
ISBN: 978-1-7345646-1-7 (e-book)

Cover design by Robin Singletary
Interior design by Madison Lux

I dedicate this book to my husband and son.

Without you, my cup would be empty. Thank you for your love, support, and understanding. You are my inspiration and reasons for being. I'm so glad I get to Live, Laugh, Love, and Learn everyday with you!

CONTENTS

CHAPTER ONE

Why You Need the Full-Plate Detox

PICTURE THIS. YOUR ALARM breaks through the quietness of your rest, and you turn it off with a smile. After seven and a half peaceful hours of sleep, you are ready to conquer the day. You say a prayer of thanksgiving and take the time to do your daily devotion, followed by a few minutes of mindful reflection. After your morning coffee and a healthy breakfast, you check your schedule. You're excited about your agenda and what you've prioritized for the day. You head out the door with a bounce in your step and gratitude in your heart.

At this point, you might be thinking, *Wow. I drag myself out of bed every day and cringe at the pile-up of things on my to-do list.* You find it hard to see a life, much less a day, where things seem to fall into place once you open your eyes. I know this scenario feels like a dream or fantasy, but what if it were possible?

What if, instead of constantly being stressed out and frazzled and chasing your tail, you could end the day, satisfied with all the things you've accomplished? What if living on the hamster wheel, running from one appointment to the next, feeling burnt out and drained, doesn't have to be *your* life? *What if?*

Yes, it's a dream—one that is easily within your reach. You just need to clear your plate.

As women, we take on everyone else's burdens. We proudly wear our Super SHEro capes and brag about how much we are juggling. When we are younger, the fire in our belly is enough to allow us to keep up with the crazy busy schedule, but as we become older and take on more responsibilities, we reach our tipping point. As life becomes more complicated, our stressors increase. Instead of taking items off our plates, we let them pile up until we feel overwhelmed and are ready to give up. When we let the pile grow, we stress ourselves out because we are not balanced. We chase balance, and instead of realizing that it's not possible, we convince ourselves that we're supposedly not as good as the next person.

Sound familiar? You are not alone. The most successful and buttoned-up women we know have at one time or another struggled with the same challenges to fit it all in, be the Super SHEro in everyone else's life, and look great while doing it. It's not easy being a Super SHEro!

As women, we are the healers, caretakers, teachers, soothers, chauffeurs, accountants, and the (fill in the blank _____). We take on too much. We become so depleted that we don't have anything left to give. We can't see a path forward. It's time for a reality check.

A 2017 study conducted in the United Kingdom by The Physiological Society explored how people react to stressors.[1] They were building upon the 1967 Holmes and Rahe Stress study, which has been widely referenced over the years.[2] While the 2017 study focused on a British demographic, their findings seem applicable and recognizable across the globe: Women consistently report higher levels of stress than male respondents.

Do you want to know how much stress you're juggling? Just do a quick Google search for the Holmes and Rahe Stress Inventory.[3] You can take the inventory to rate how much stress you're dealing with. It's mind-blowing. Being honest will help you understand why you have to get a handle on your crazy-busy life now.

In researching stress levels for women, I did a little jig when I read studies that confirm what I've heard before—women have more active brains than men.[4] Let me say this: This is not a man-bashing book. I respect, honor, and recognize that we have a lot of men out there who wear their capes too. While I am focused on how we *all* can improve the way we work, I have a particular empathy for the plight of the Super SHEro (no offense to the fellows).

Back to that study about our brain activity. After analyzing more than forty thousand brain scans, a study by the *Journal of Alzheimer's Disease*, found that the brains of female subjects were more active in key areas and overall.[5] Boom! Female brains showed more activity in the pre-frontal cortex that impacts focus, organizing, time management, the regulation of emotions, the understanding of different points of view, and other executive functions. Think of it as your brain's CEO. Our brains are doing more. No wonder we are so stressed out.

Our brains are in overdrive, and we are giving so much to others that we don't have anything left for ourselves. Consider this information from a study commissioned by Welch's of more than two thousand American moms: The average mom puts in a ninety-eight-hour work week after you add up all the hours that she puts in for her family after a full day in the workplace![6] Moms are working fourteen-hour days. Like you, many feel that they are just dealing with on-going lists of tasks. The final shocker from this study was that most moms reported only having about an hour and seven minutes of time to themselves per day. (I don't know if they counted Target runs and bathroom time.)

Wouldn't it be great to do something for yourself without feeling as if you are "should-ing"? You know, should-ing: I should volunteer, I should join that group, I should be happy with where I am in life. Wouldn't it be great to shed the should-ing and guilt and enjoy your alone time again?

If you've been should-ing on yourself, you need a detox: a full-plate detox.

Get Ready for the Full-Plate Detox

A detox is a focused effort over a short period of time to help remove unhealthy stuff from your life. We're used to thinking of a detox for junk food or trashy TV. For our purposes, we are going to focus on how you can detox your time and your energy.

In many cases, the unhealthy stuff that we need to remove is the false belief that we can continue to push ourselves to the limit and not suffer for it. We have to remove the notion that we can put our brains and emotions into overdrive and keep on giving joyfully and abundantly to others.

In order to achieve the dream that I painted a picture of at the start of this chapter, you have to be seriously committed to ditch being overwhelmed, and shed the guilt and unhealthy beliefs in order to get back to the top of your priority list.

Speaking from experience, I know it's not easy, which is why I created the full-plate detox (TFPD). The process and activities that I will lay out for you in this book are designed to help you kick the ineffective time-management habits that are creating unnecessary stress in your life *and* help you shift into a more intentional lifestyle full of what you love.

The full-plate detox is about giving yourself permission to let go of what's weighing you down. It's about stepping off the hamster wheel and slowing down in order to move forward. I can't lie and tell you that it won't be challenging or that parts of this process won't feel uncomfortable. I *can* tell you that if you stick it out it will be worth it.

I used to be a proud member of the night-owl club. When I started my own business, I burned both ends of the candle and waved that flag proudly. I came from an industry where deadlines ran our days and working overtime meant going over budget. I carried that mindset with me and set unrealistic deadlines and schedules for myself, trying to keep up with expectations about what a successful entrepreneur should be. When I had my son, it went from bad to worse. I was struggling to care for a newborn, grow a new business, and meet client needs while still being a wife, sister, friend, daughter, and auntie. I was on the road to burn out.

In this book, I share strategies that I had to put in place when I finally got fed up with being sick and tired of being overwhelmed. Through research, crying fits, and trial and error, I've created a system that works for me. When I find that life is getting crazy, I check in to see what part of my routine needs an adjustment. I have used these same strategies with my private coaching clients, and I've taught them to hundreds in my training classes. My clients have told me they work. Class attendees have reconnected with me and told me that these strategies work. If you give this process an honest try and tweak it to suit your life, they'll work for you too!

To help you in your journey, I'll be sharing a few stories in the book (with some changes to names and details to protect privacy) and also telling you about the strategies I practice myself. Let's get you on board.

In order for the full-plate detox to work, you will have to let go of some concepts you may have accepted as truth without thinking about them. Among the first of many is the concept of time management.

Time Management Is a Myth

We all get 84,600 seconds a day, 1,440 minutes, twenty-four hours. Time is a non-renewable commodity. We can't beg, borrow, or steal it, no matter what the poets say. Our belief that we can actually manage or influence time is part of our problem. We all have a set amount of time each day: twenty-four hours.

The phrase "time management" falsely leads us to believe that we can control time. When we can't, we become anxious because we think we're terrible at this important life skill and end up feeling overwhelmed.

Instead of time management, we have to shift our thinking to energy investment. We can't control time, but we can make better choices about what we do with our time. We can't get more time, but we can choose to schedule fewer activities in the time we have available to us. We can't turn back time, but we *can* choose to make smarter choices with the time we have in front of us.

Choose Wisely

When I was growing up, my father had several nicknames for me (very typical in Jamaican families). One was "Wingie." The nice way to translate it was that I was very skinny. I had a hard time gaining weight well into my adult life. (No, I'm not bragging; this came with its own challenges.) After several health challenges and the birth of my son, I started to put on weight. Those who knew me from my early days noticed the difference. I didn't stress about the weight gain as much as I did about the impact on my strength and mobility. I committed to making changes.

As a former gymnast and martial artist, I was no stranger to working out. I knew how to sweat it out and got myself back in the gym. But I quickly found out that exercising the old way wasn't working out for the new me. I had to learn how to work out without injuring my older body. And when the inevitable happened, I had to learn how to work out *with* an injury. I still wasn't seeing the change I wanted. Since I always had the opposite problem, I now needed to learn how to lose weight instead of gaining it. I had to shift from a lifetime of behavior. (Truth: I'm still working on it.)

It wasn't until I did a fitness challenge and was given a meal plan by a nutritionist that I realized how much I had to learn. The nutritionist said something to me that was music to my ears: There were no right or wrong foods, just smart or dumb choices. He also told me he could write me a plan that included Twinkies and chocolate cake, but it probably wouldn't be the smartest choice to reach my goals. Too much of anything—no matter how good it is—isn't good for you.

As I'm still learning with food (I love chocolate) and as you'll learn in this book, we always have choices. We choose what's on our plate. We choose how many things we add to our task list. We say yes when we should say no. We guilt ourselves into overcommitting until we burn out. *But* we can make different choices that will help us reach our goals, and if we don't like the direction our choice takes us, we can make a new one.

Why You Should Stop Chasing Balance

Chasing the dream doesn't have to burn us out. It's time for us to quit chasing balance. Constantly striving to balance everything is one of our biggest stressors. I attended a conference a few years ago that opened my eyes. The conference keynote speaker was Dan Thurmon, author of an awesome book, *Off Balance on Purpose: Embrace Uncertainty and Create a Life You Love.*[7] Before I attended his session, I used to say that I helped my clients achieve balance and kept trying to reach balance myself.

Through talented juggling and an insightful message, he taught us that we should give up chasing balance because we can't give equal attention to everything on our plate. Instead, we should be intentional about what we are juggling, tossing some things higher than others so we can focus on the right things at the right time. When we try to give everything our attention without setting the right intentions, we are *off balance and off purpose.* When we make the conscious choice about what areas of our lives will get more of our energy than others, we are *off balance* but *on purpose.* The trick isn't to chase balance. The trick is to chase purpose.

Once you focus on controlling your activities and give up trying to control time, you will see a greater impact in the areas that matter most.

I know you are busy, and it might feel like tackling the full-plate detox is just one more thing to add to your to-do list. I'm asking you to trust the process and give yourself permission to get back to the top of your priority list. The full-plate detox will help you get the clarity you need to stop feeling overwhelmed. I hope this chapter has helped set the stage for your detox and has motivated you to see it through.

I want you to commit right now to following through with the process. Give yourself permission and the time you'll need to get back to the top of your priority list.

To seal the deal, go and look at yourself in the mirror and say, "I need to do a full-plate detox. I deserve to be at the top of my priority list. I promise to see this detox through."

Focus Tasks

Throughout the book, I will ask you to do a little work called Focus Tasks, which will guide you through implementing the strategies I'll teach you. To make this process easier for you, I've created an electronic workbook with Focus Sheets that you can download and use as you complete the activities in this book. Get your copy of the electronic workbook *The Full-Plate Detox Study Guide* and other resources in the Full-Plate Detox Group on Facebook at www.facebook.com/groups/ FullPlateDetox. You'll be able to hang out with other detoxers and check in with me for guidance and accountability.

FOCUS TASK #1
Why You Need a Detox

Why do you need a full-plate detox right now?

CHAPTER TWO

Stop Trying to Pour from an Empty Cup

WE'VE ALL HEARD OR said the phrase, "You can't pour from an empty cup." Unfortunately, we say the phrase, shrug our shoulders, and walk away as if that statement by itself is the magic answer. We don't stop and ask why we keep trying to pour from that empty cup, how our cup gets empty in the first place, and better yet, how we can fill it up again.

Our Empty Energy Cup

Over the past couple of years, I've had many class attendees and coaching clients tell me they are struggling with an empty cup. The theme of an empty cup has popped up in so many seminars, conversations, and events that I began to think of it as "the phrase." Based on my conversations, when folks refer to the "empty cup," they are really talking about their energy. Now, when I think of "the phrase," I picture a cup emptied of energy and resources.

As I spoke with more people and asked more questions, I realized a few things:

1. **Many women feel overwhelmed and drained**. When I host events and classes, I ask those who feel overwhelmed to raise their hands. Almost every hand in the room goes up. I've yet to have someone tell me they can put more on their plate. Everyone feels like they are juggling too many things and don't have any energy left to take on more tasks.

2. **Women struggle with different things.** While we all deal with common themes, such as family issues, workload, or financial problems, different struggles often leave us drained. What's draining their cup of energy depends on the issues they're tackling at the moment, where they are in their life cycle, and their available resources.

3. **People would do things differently if they knew how.** Not one person that says "the phrase" wants their situation to stay the same. Each person wants circumstances to change but hasn't taken steps toward making changes, usually because they don't know where to start.

After I encountered so many people who were struggling with the same issues, I hosted an online summit called "Fill Your Empty Cup." I pulled together more than twenty experts from a variety of industries to share strategies to improve our careers, productivity, health, wellness, and mindsets. The interviews were mind-blowing and inspiring, but I realized that they were just the tip of the iceberg. The summit felt like a drop in the bucket or cup, if you will. While the experts all showed up and shared amazing insights and tips, I realized that I wanted to do more to provide ongoing support, encouragement, and strategies to the hundreds of people who signed up to fill their empty cups.

One thing I've learned is that you can't just attend a workshop, listen to an interview, wave a magic wand, and have overflowing cups. You have to do some soul searching and put in the work to learn how to fill your cup up—again and again.

While you feel energized in the moment, if you don't put in the time to uncover the root cause of your empty cup, it's like eating a sugary snack when you're starving. It's not filling and doesn't truly satisfy your hunger.

The Link Between Empty Energy Cups and Full Plates

My quest to figure out why we all have empty energy cups led me to the notion of having a full plate. As I spoke with people about where they were investing their time, I noticed a key difference between two groups of people. Those who complained that their plates were full were busy with activities that didn't satisfy their goals. Those who were working on activities that were in alignment with their goals admitted that they were busy, but they thrived on what they were doing.

The key is that when we are busy with activities that just pass the time, our energy levels and our cups become drained and depleted. By contrast, when we are doing what brings us joy and satisfaction, we feel energized.

Are you pouring your energy into everyone and everything else without leaving anything for yourself?

Think about your day as a nine-ounce cup. Like that cup, we can't expand the day. Nine ounces is nine ounces. You can only put so much in the container before it overflows. Unlike the cup, we can't just fill the day back up with more time, so as we discussed in the previous chapter, we have to make choices about what we do with our time.

When your energy cup is empty, you have to think about how you can fill it back up. If you continue doing the same things, your cup will remain empty, because those energy drains on your plate will keep you depleted.

In the next chapter, I will dive deeper into what a full plate is, but for now, think of your schedule as a plate. When our schedule is taken over by mindless tasks, commitments to others, and activities that don't align with our goals, we are busy, but we are not accomplishing what we really want. When our schedule is dedicated to what is aligned with our goals, we feel good about our day. If you put the right things on your plate, you'll be fulfilled and energized. If you put the wrong things on your plate, you'll be drained.

If your calendar is filled with activities for everyone else and none for yourself, you need to take a lesson from the safety lecture given at the start of flights: Put your own oxygen mask on first. On a flight, you have about fifteen to eighteen seconds of consciousness before you pass out if the pressure drops below thirty-seven thousand feet.[8] If you don't put on your oxygen mask, you probably can't help a loved one.

Our day-to-day lives function in the same manner. If you are over-committed and don't take care of yourself by devoting time to what energizes you, you won't be able to give to others. If you put the right things on your plate, you'll be fulfilled, energized, and better equipped to support others.

When our cups are drained, it's impossible for us to continue giving at the same level that we would like to. You'll find it difficult to give anything the attention and energy you want to. It's important to figure out what *is* draining your cup in the first place, get the energy drains off your plate, and then replace them with the right activities.

The Hidden Energy Cup Drains

Remember my conversations with people about what was draining them? I had the opportunity to go deep with a few people, and while they were dealing with issues that we can all relate to (work, family, money problems, etc.), other underlying issues were even bigger stumbling blocks.

Some of the biggest energy drains weren't what we could see physically; it was the mental turmoil that folks were going through. As I share those with you, please keep an honest record of how many you may be dealing with. True reflection on our *real* issues is the only way to get more of what we want.

Negative self-talk and doubts: According to the Huffington Post UK, we have an average of fifty thousand to seventy thousand thoughts per day.[9] That's thirty-five thoughts per minute. Other studies claim that up to 70 percent of our thoughts are negative self-talk.[10] Your inner critic (we'll call her Negative Nelly) is notorious for whispering nasty thoughts to you that you would never say to another person. These negative thoughts set you up for failure by creating self-doubt. When you doubt yourself, you hold yourself back from achieving your goals and waste time comparing yourself to others while creating unrealistic expectations.

Although the specific source is uncertain, a quote attributed to Frank Outlaw addresses the power of our thoughts:

"Watch your thoughts, for they become words.
Watch your words, for they become actions.
Watch your actions, for they become habits.
Watch your habits, for they become character.
Watch your character, for it becomes your destiny."[11]

Limiting beliefs and expectations: I learned something interesting about fleas—and us—from Steve Harvey's book, *Act Like a Success, Think Like a Success*.[12] He shares a story about fleas that are kept in a jar. The fleas, which have a natural ability to jump almost three feet, learn to jump only as high as the jar allows without hitting their heads. If the fleas reproduce in the jar, their babies will do the same, even though they have the ability to jump higher. A scientist did an experiment with fleas in a box. When he put them in the box, they jumped out. He then put a sheet of glass over the top of the box. At first, the fleas kept trying to jump out, but eventually stopped because they were hitting the glass. But when the scientist eventually removed the sheet of glass, the fleas *gave up* trying to jump out of the box!

Like those fleas, our limiting beliefs stop us from achieving our natural abilities. The expectations that you set for yourself will influence how high you reach, how much you put on your plate, and how fast you drain your cup. Have you stopped trying because of your beliefs?

Is your vision of productivity running around and staying busy? Are you confusing busyness and activity with accomplishment? Do you think that you have to go faster and do more in order to "be successful?" Consider how the limiting thoughts and beliefs that you have regarding productivity and being successful are impacting your energy.

Fear of failure: None of us like to fail. As children, we were quick to go for what we wanted without worrying about failing. As we grew older, we worried about failure. We worry so much that we start playing safe and stop trying new things. Playing it safe, small, and only doing what's in our comfort zone might keep us from avoiding failure, but it will also keep us from experiencing the joy of achieving new goals.

Failure doesn't define you. Failure is not who you are. Think of past failures as stepping stones to your success. Thomas Edison had one thousand unsuccessful attempts at inventing the lightbulb. He was asked how he felt about failing one thousand times. He reportedly replied: "I didn't fail one thousand times. The light bulb was an invention with one thousand steps."[13] Flip the script and start thinking of failure as just another step on your path to success.

Lack of confidence and suffering from imposter syndrome: Those who suffer from a psychological term called "imposter syndrome" lack confidence and believe that who they are and what they do just isn't good enough. This shows up in behavior patterns.

As women, we have a bad habit of just assuming we're not good enough for whatever we're facing. I'll let you in on a secret; it's highly likely that you and most of the women you work with have battled imposter syndrome at one time or another. While you think you're the only one dealing with it, you're not alone. It's a common challenge experienced by amazing Super SHEros everywhere.

Yes. *YOU ARE NOT ALONE.* Sorry for yelling, but this is important.

As a high achiever, from the outside looking in, you've got the life. You're out and about, climbing that ladder, wearing the right clothes and you're *scared* they'll figure out you're making it up as you go along. You (and just about every other woman that you pass by) suffer from the imposter syndrome. You feel like a fraud and as if others are judging you and finding you lacking. You have to let go of self-limiting beliefs that you're not good enough and that you're a fraud so you can own your power.

Our habitual responses to stress: Earlier, we identified that women tend to deal with more stress and that we have more active brains. We learn to cope and make it through the day. The ways we cope with stress can drain us or energize us. I don't remember where I first heard the "Carrots, Eggs, or Coffee Bean" parable, but it was life-changing for me. If you haven't heard it, read on.

> A young woman went to her mother and told her about her life and how things were so hard for her. She did not know how she was going to make it and wanted to give up. She was tired of fighting and struggling. It seemed as one problem was solved, a new one arose.
>
> Her mother took her to the kitchen. She filled three pots with water and placed each on a high fire. Soon the pots came to boil. In the first she placed carrots, in the second she placed eggs and in the last she placed ground coffee beans. She let them sit and boil, without saying a word.
>
> In about twenty minutes she turned off the burners. She fished the carrots out and placed them in a bowl. She pulled the eggs out and placed them in a bowl.
>
> Then she ladled the coffee out and placed it in a bowl. Turning to her daughter, she asked, "Tell me what you see."

"Carrots, eggs, and coffee," she replied.

Her mother brought her closer and asked her to feel the carrots. She did and noted that they were soft. The mother then asked the daughter to take an egg and break it. After pulling off the shell, she observed the hard-boiled egg. Finally, the mother asked the daughter to sip the coffee. The daughter smiled, as she tasted its rich aroma the daughter then asked, "What does it mean, mother?"

Her mother explained that each of these objects had faced the same adversity: boiling water. Each reacted differently. The carrot went in strong, hard and unrelenting. However, after being subjected to the boiling water, it softened and became weak. The egg had been fragile. Its thin outer shell had protected its liquid interior, but after sitting through the boiling water, its insides became hardened. The ground coffee beans were unique, however. After they were in the boiling water, they had changed the water.

"Which are you?" she asked her daughter. "When adversity knocks on your door, how do you respond? Are you a carrot, an egg or a coffee bean?"[14]

How you respond to stress can either help you refill your energy cup or drain it more quickly. Are you a carrot, egg, or coffee bean?

Know Your Hidden Energy Cup Drains

As you read through the hidden energy cup drains, did you take note of how many are you struggling with? Don't beat yourself up if you identified with most of them. Remember I said I am sharing the struggles I've overcome and the proven strategies I've learned to combat them in this book. Yes, I've dealt with negative self-talk, limiting beliefs, imposter syndrome, fear of failure, and letting adversity negatively change me. I had to learn to let it all go and do my best to change the water and not let circumstances keep me down.

My goal in asking you to think about this is so that you can start looking at the areas of your life that you can control and see what specific things, people, and activities are stressing you out so that you can change the water.

I want to encourage you to give yourself guilt-free permission to stop trying to pour from an empty cup. In order to reach that point, you have to honestly reflect and explore the habits, mindsets, and behaviors that are keeping you from moving forward.

FOCUS TASK #2
What's Draining Your Cup?

On the Focus Sheets, answer the following questions:

> » What are you should-ing on yourself about that you need to let go? What do you feel guilty about?
> » What does Negative Nelly keep whispering in your head?
> » What beliefs or expectations do you have that are contributing to feeling overwhelmed?
> » How do you respond to stressful situations (like the carrot, egg, or coffee bean)?
> » Do certain situations make you more fragile/hardened?
> » What imposter syndrome beliefs do you need to let go of?
> » Where do you shine and thrive? What are you are good at, and what areas do others turn to you for help?

Before you turn the page…
Please don't just answer these questions quickly in your head and

then flip the page. One thing I've learned from working with my private clients is that you won't see results if you don't ask and answer the difficult questions. Remember your promise at the end of the first chapter to see this detox through. That means you will keep yourself at the top of your priority list and do the hard work.

Go grab your pen and focus on you.

CHAPTER THREE

What's on Your Plate?

FIRST THINGS FIRST—GIVE YOURSELF a high five and a pat on the back for committing to the full-plate detox and pushing through the last chapter. If you honestly answered the questions at the end of the last chapter, then you might be feeling a little discouraged right now. Don't "should" on yourself! It can be easy to slip into a pity party, which was not the point of those questions. Think of the last chapter and the work we'll do in this chapter as opening up a wound to let out the infection. Once we get rid of the infection and poison, we can get to the healing.

You should now have a clearer picture about some of the activities and beliefs that have been draining your energy cup. Now it's time to gain clarity on what's taking up your time in each area of your life. We will break down what's working and what needs improving and start thinking of replacements for what is getting in your way.

In this chapter, the rubber starts to meet the road.

Earlier, we acknowledged that on any given day, we are dealing with a few of the top life stressors. Psychiatrists Thomas Holmes and Richard Rahe developed The Holmes and Rahe Stress Scale in 1967. They looked at medical records of more than five thousand patients to see if they could find causal links between stressful events and illnesses. They came up with a list of forty-three different life events and assigned them scores based upon how impactful they were on someone's quality of life.[15]

Items on the scale range from our relationships with our spouses, children, and family members to financial challenges to changes in dynamics at work or at home to personal habits and other potentially adverse events. The scale has been updated for our modern lives, but interestingly, many of the original items are still relevant to us today.

Earlier, I asked you to do a Google search for the scale and take the linked assessment. If you didn't take it yet, go ahead and do it now. Then return to this section.

FOCUS TASK #3
List Your Stressors

Are you surprised at how many major life stressors you are dealing with? Write them down in your workbook.

FOCUS TASK #4
Let's Play a Drinking Game

It's time for a reality check. I want you to do an activity that I guide people through at live events. It's designed to drive home the point about the stressors on our plates that drain and empty our energy cups.

1. Go grab a cup and fill it with water to match the level of energy you have right now. If you feel like you are running on 75 percent of energy, fill the cup up three-fourths of the way with water.
2. Drink water to correspond to each of your stressors:
   - One sip if it is only a little problem
   - Two sips if it's a growing problem
   - Three big gulps if the stressor is one of your biggest stressors.

Did you make it through your entire list before you emptied your cup? How quickly did your energy cup drain out? How quickly do you become drained in your day-to-day life?

You may not have realized how much of what has happened to you has impacted you.

That's one key sign of a Super SHEro. You have become so used to the stressors and reacting like a carrot or an egg, that you probably haven't considered just how heavy the load is that you've been lifting. This is a common characteristic of all the Super SHEros that I've worked with: Accepting life's challenges as an inevitable part of their journey without considering alternatives to carrying the load.

Now that you have clarity on what is draining you, you are ready to start creating your action plan to minimize the problems and create your healthy plate.

Know What's on Your Plate

Having a full plate isn't a bad thing. We want to be satisfied in our day-to-day lives. You may have noticed the analogy between our eating habits and the full-plate detox by now. I wanted to use something basic that we could *all* identify with: food. We all eat. We all understand the concept that some things we eat are healthier for us than others. We can all identify with that bloated feeling that comes after gorging ourselves on a huge holiday meal. I'm also sure we can identify with how hard it is to change our eating habits when they are having a negative impact on our health.

It's the same with our time. In this book, when I talk about a full plate and choosing a healthier plate, I'm talking about your schedule and the choices that you make about where you invest your time. A healthy plate is a schedule with a mix of daily obligations and necessities along with a good dose of inspiring, spine-tingling, goal-getting activities. A healthy-plate day starts out like the morning I described at the start of the book. An unhealthy-plate is a day that is stressful and demotivating.

For example, when my client Julia and I started working together, she was burned out. While she loved her job as an analyst, she was working in a very stressful environment. When she came home, she just wanted to decompress, but her evening hours weren't her own. When we looked at all the things on her plate, she realized that she was over-committed. She was serving on the membership committee for a local group, gave up what little time she had to the school PTA, and spent time on the phone with a friend who kept making bad choices and then complained about it. Julia felt guilty for saying "no" to all these commitments. She had the best of intentions and wanted to help, but she had nothing left for herself. She wanted to have more fun in her life and felt weighed down.

We worked to fix what was on her plate. In the end, she realized that while she liked the idea of volunteering, she didn't want to be stuck dealing with paperwork and committee politics in her free time. She craved more fun, laughter, and physical activity in her life. After exploring what she enjoyed, she decided to become a Zumba instructor and volunteer her time having fun, getting healthy, and teaching classes.

By picking up this book, you have acknowledged—at least to yourself—that you are feeling overwhelmed from dealing with all the things on your plate. Now take a moment to identify what you crave.

Let's *Make* Room for What You Crave

In the words of Steven Covey, "The key is not to **prioritize** what's on **your schedule**, but to **schedule your priorities**."[16] You have to put your priorities on your schedule first and then plan the rest of your day around it.

If you are not on your own calendar, you are not on your own priority list. It's not enough to set goals and say you want to get things done. You have to create the space and time to actually work on your goals.

Let me share a story with you. Another client, Liz, wanted to go back to school to complete a certification. She was single when she completed her last certification but was struggling five years later to fit it in with a new job, husband, and toddler. She kept saying she didn't have the time. So I asked her to think about how much time per week she would need to devote to her certification. When she worked it out, she really only needed to set aside about seven hours to study, do assignments, and attend classes. Next, I had her analyze her time investment for the next week to see where she could free up those seven hours. When we next spoke, she had "found" a total of eleven hours during the week that she could re-allocate to working on her goal. Once the time barrier was removed, moving forward was no longer a problem.

The point is that you have to take some activities off your calendar and look at where you are spending your time in order to make room for more of what you want. You may not even realize where time gets "lost". For example, working on new tasks often takes longer than we plan because we don't really know how long it will take.

In order to create a clean healthy plate, you have to know your time wasters and ditch the junk. Time wasters are activities and habits that suck the life out of you and your schedule. Here's a partial list of some common time wasters: procrastination, email, meetings, slow-decision making, lack of focus, lack of communication skills, socializing, social media, disorganization, over-commitment, not using a calendar, not being tech savvy, and not organizing your work.

Like the hidden energy cup drains, it's hard to see these time wasters coming, but they add up. When you start paying attention to how you are investing your time, you'll notice that you have "lost time" on your calendar that you have spent on unplanned or unimportant things. Instead, we have to pay attention to the hidden time wasters and track where your time is going.

FOCUS TASK #5
Time Log

Complete a daily log and track how you are spending your time. You can do this for the entire day or just at work. For example, yesterday, look at how long it took you to complete tasks and if you originally budgeted enough time for them. Track your time in thirty-minute chunks. The sample below is a guide.

Activity	Time that it Took	Planned on Your Schedule? (Yes/No)	Time Waster (Yes/No)
Read articles on productivity— got distracted trying to install apps they recommended on my phone.	60 minutes	No	Mostly yes
Went on LinkedIn to update my profile. Had to look up job descriptions from past jobs.	90 minutes	Yes, but took longer than planned	No

I'll warn you, tracking where your time is currently going won't be your favorite activity in this book, but it is necessary. You can't change what you don't measure.

One last thought from Steven Covey: "The main thing is to keep the main thing, the main thing."[17] Take each Focus Task and the strategies that you implement as a stepping stone to your own unique success plan and just do one thing at a time.

Remember your goal in this chapter is to better understand what's on your plate so you can make room for what you are truly craving.

The Pareto Principle or the 80/20 Rule

One of the single most important strategies that helps me maintain my sanity is based on The Pareto Principle, often called the 80/20 rule.[18]

I first heard about this when I worked as a marketing manager in New York. A sales guy shared that he gets 80 percent of his sales from 20 percent of his customers. The Pareto Principle is named after an Italian economist-sociologist, Vilfredo Pareto. He observed the relationship between different items. For example, he noted that 80 percent of the land in Italy was owned by only 20 percent of the population. In applying this observation, we understand that a smaller percentage (20 percent) of a group or activity has a larger impact (80 percent) on the result.

Think about it this way: 20 percent of what you do will give you 80 percent of your results. Conversely, 80 percent of what you do will only give you 20 percent of your results.

When you think about what's on your plate and try to make room for what you crave, you might not need as much time as you think you do. You may only need to let go of a few things or eliminate a few of your time wasters to make enough room on your calendar for what you crave.

FOCUS TASK #6
Block out time to apply the 80/20 Rule.

Try to find 20 percent of your calendar to devote to what you crave (20 percent of an average eight-hour day is ninety-six minutes). Your goal is to identify about ninety minutes of your day to commit to whatever goal you decide to work on.

Find Your Unique Viewpoint

You've probably been on a quest to find your productivity rhythm for a while. I'm sure you've tried a number of things that you've read about or that your friends have tried. The reason they haven't worked is because your viewpoint and perspective are unique.

There is no cookie-cutter solution that will magically fix all your problems. Just because an app, tool, or idea works for someone else, doesn't mean it will work for you. You need to really think about what you want and your unique path to getting there. There is no one path for everyone, and there will be some things that you can't change or control.

As you implement each focus task, you'll be creating a unique plan for yourself. For some of my clients, implementing one focus task did the trick. Others have had to layer different strategies. And yet others had to make further adjustments as their situations changed.

Your life viewpoints are the different lenses or focal points through which you view life. Understanding what you want for each viewpoint and knowing how they impact each other will help you create a successful action plan.

The SWOT Analysis

When I went to graduate school in Boston, I was introduced to the beauty of the SWOT Analysis. I learned SWOT stood for **S**trengths, **W**eaknesses, **O**pportunities, and **T**hreats in my Marketing Strategies class. We were taught to create a matrix and use it to identify each of these four items as we tried to position our product in the market place.

This strategic planning technique helped us create objectives and an action plan. It became second nature for me to use this approach whenever I had a problem that needed to be solved.

When it comes to your goal of creating a healthier plate or schedule, we need to analyze your current plate and all areas of your life.

FOCUS TASK #7
SWOT Your Way Around Your Full Plate

In coaching, we use a tool called the Wheel of Life, but to stay in theme, your task is to SWOT your way around your full plate by taking a look at life viewpoints: family, career, finances, health, spirituality, relationships, personal development, recreation, and education.

It's helpful to consider the strengths and weaknesses as what you bring to the table and control and think about opportunities and threats as external influences that you might not be able to control.

For each area, identify your unique situations.

Strengths: What advantages, resources, tools, skills, habits, or traits do you have for each area that will help you be successful?

Weaknesses: What are the possible drawbacks; bad habits; or lack of skills, resources, or tools that might create obstacles to your success?

Opportunities: What's going on around you that you can leverage to help you reach your goal? Think about people, services, commitments, and obligations.

Threats: What's going on around you that might impact you as you work on your goal? Think about people, services, commitments, obligations, and time drains that can hold you back.

Do one SWOT matrix for each area of your life. If you feel overwhelmed trying to do the SWOT for all the areas of your life, pick the ones that are troubling you the most. To figure this out, rate your satisfaction for each area on a scale of 1–10, with 1=not satisfied and 10=very satisfied. Start with the areas that are 5 or lower.

When filling out the form, go with your gut. You can always add to it later. For example, when Brenda started her SWOT analysis, one big area of dissatisfaction was her overall health. See her health SWOT as follows:

HEALTH (satisfaction rating: 4)	
Strengths	**Weaknesses**
I don't have any illnesses I can physically work out I used to run when I was in high school	I don't like working out on my own I never stick with a routine unless someone makes me do it
Opportunities	**Threats**
My best friend asked me to sign up for a 5k We live close enough to run together	I hate running in the cold, and it's getting colder. How can I stick to the training plan when it's cold outside?

Please don't skip this step. Your SWOT analysis will be your launch pad for getting more of what you are truly craving!

CHAPTER FOUR

Get Vision Clarity to Satisfy Your Cravings

FOCUS. GET CLARITY. Have vision. You've said these words before. Others have told you that this is the secret to achieving your goals. When you focus on something, you make it the center of your interest or activity, letting nothing else in. Vision clarity means you can picture what you want so clearly that you have no doubt about what you will achieve. It's crystal clear.

Logically, you understand the concept of focus and vision clarity. Although it is a challenge, vision clarity is a key component of satisfying your cravings and reaching your goals. But how do you get there, and why does it matter in the full-plate detox?

One big challenge to being intentional about what we put on our plate is that we are not really sure what we're working toward. We tend to chase ideas and goals like shiny new objects because we become caught up in what we think we should do and in what others are doing. We lack vision clarity.

This chapter is about helping you focus on your vision and creating a list of potential goals in alignment with your vision.

Setting Your Vision Coordinates

There's a great quote by the Cheshire Cat in Alice in Wonderland. "If you don't know where you're going, then any road will get you there."[19] When you don't have a particular destination in mind, then you can wander down any road, and you'll still go somewhere. Successful organizations and businesses work on plans with clear visions and goals. I have found it very useful to apply the same methodology to how we plan our personal lives.

One of the best gifts I ever received was a GPS unit. This was back in the day before our cell phones started doing everything for us. I had just started my business as an organizing consultant and found myself traveling around Long Island, New York. I grew up in the city, so most of the roads were unfamiliar to me. My husband knew the area like the back of his hand, but since he had a day job, I had to figure out how to navigate on my own.

Needless to say, I got lost a few times. I had to add extra travel time as a cushion in case I got lost. I felt stressed out each time I had to see a new client. I realized that I became selective about the clients that I served to minimize this stress. And then my husband gifted me with a GPS. My very own stand-alone navigator. It was a game changer for me. All I had to do was plug in my destination, and it took me there, on time and stress-free.

Vision clarity is like plugging in an address in the GPS unit; it tells you where to go. To reach that amazing place where you are rocking your goals and making it look easy, you need a clear picture of where you're going.

Your vision focuses your energy, actions, behaviors, and decisions toward what is most important to you.

It is a personal mission statement of what you want to accomplish and how you want to be remembered. Start by writing it down. Your vision has to be clear enough for you to explain to others. It doesn't have to be a book. Keep it focused so that you can easily recognize when your activities are in alignment. If you haven't written down your vision, that's the first place to start.

FOCUS TASK #8
Write Your Vision Statement

Use this template to write your vision statement. I learned of it years ago. Just fill in the blanks.

> I want to (what you want to achieve, do, or become) so that (reasons why it is important). I will do this by (specific actions you'll take to reach your goal). I value (list three of your values) because (why these values are important to you). So I will (what you can do to live by these values). I want to be known by (an important person/group) as someone who is (qualities you want to have).

Here's an example of a personal vision statement using the template:

> I want to be known as someone who walks her talk so that my family and friends will respect me. I will do this by being present and intentional about where I invest my time. I value honesty, working hard, and appreciating my blessings because showing gratitude and being trustworthy are important character traits. So I will always try to be authentic, honest, and prioritize the important things in life. I want to be known by my family, clients, and friends as someone who is purposeful, trustworthy, credible, and efficient.

Notice the first sentence. I can memorize that and walk away with it as my guide post. The rest of the paragraph reinforces this and keeps me connected to my "why."

Okay, now it's your turn. If your vision statement doesn't flow in one sitting, start by identifying the values that are important to you. List the people who are most important to you and how you want them to remember you. Keep running the words through your head as you go until it feels right. By the way, you're a whole person, so your statement can include both personal and work goals.

Put Your Brain to Work

Now that your vision is in writing, it's time to leverage the power of your brain to work on visualizing your goals. Your brain is wired to work with visual images. Writing down our goals is one key to success, but so is the ability to visualize them. A study led by Elinor Amit showed that people create visual images as they are thinking.[20] They can better recall information associated with visualization and vivid images. Visualization is one of the most powerful goal achievement techniques you have in your arsenal. Research has shown that one of the many benefits of visualization is the increased likelihood of success.

When athletes visualize successfully hitting a free throw, they engage their muscles, along with their minds, to mentally practice success. Australian psychologist Alan Richardson conducted a study with a basketball team on the impact of mental rehearsal (visualization) techniques in sports.[21] He split basketball players into three groups and tested each group on how many free throws they could make. One group practiced free throws for twenty minutes a day for five days. The second group had a professional guide them through visualizing making free throws, and the third (control) group was asked not to even think about basketball.

When the groups were tested again after four weeks, the first group had a 24 percent improvement in their free throws. The second group realized a 23 percent increase just from visualization, and the third group saw no change in their success. Visualization, by itself, is proven to improve performance, but we won't stop there.

Purposeful visualization of achieving your goal uses the power of your mind to boost success. Purposeful visualization engages not just your visual sense but incorporates all the other senses so that what you are visualizing is as real as possible. Don't just picture what you want. Think of what you'll hear when you hit your goal. What will you say?

How will you feel when you reach your goal? Think about the emotions you'll experience. Visualizing the activity from the first person and seeing the action through your own eyes will make it more real.

The Power of a Vision Board

If you've never created a vision board, I'm sure you've heard of one by now. If you haven't experienced it for yourself, a vision board is basically a collage of images that you choose to represent your goals. It's designed by you to showcase what you want to achieve.

I admit, at first, I was a sceptic. I couldn't get excited about the whole concept of cutting and pasting because I seem to be missing the crafty gene. Then a friend introduced me to digital vision boards using online images, and the fire was lit. I love them so much now because I could more easily find images that really sparked my passions.

Whether you prefer cutting and pasting of physical paper or digital images, the point is that vision boards work to excite and motivate you to tackle your goals. They are constant, inspirational reminders about what you want to achieve.

Want to run a marathon? Pull a picture of someone crossing the finish line. Want to speak on stage? Grab a picture of your dream venue. Want to get your abs beach-body ready? Put up a picture of that slamming bikini you'll be able to wear once you hit your goals.

Your vision board will keep images of your goals front and center to remind you of what you're working toward. The vision board helps trick your brain and create familiarity with the outcome—your final goals—to make them less scary and unfamiliar. As you visualize yourself successfully overcoming obstacles and reaching your goals, you remove many of the barriers to achieving them.

Your vision board will give you daily promptings. When we have long-range goals, the finish line is further away than we'd like. A vision board will keep the outcome you're working on close at hand. The positive, fun images you choose for your vision board will help keep up your energy and motivation levels, especially when things get tough. (In case you haven't figured it out yet, one of your focus tasks will be to create your own vision board, but first let's talk about your goals.)

What's on Your Bucket List?

Too often, we whisper our secret desires inside our heads, afraid to let the world hear our deepest wishes. Saying what we crave out loud makes it real. It's time to be more intentional and plan a plate that will satisfy your cravings. Instead of wishing that you could do something, put it on your plate and figure out a path forward to take it from vision to reality. Put it on your bucket list.

You may have said or heard someone talk about items on their bucket list. These are usually something crazy, freaky, and even dangerous that someone wants to do before they kick the bucket. They might even kick the bucket while doing it. The point is, people often put the most outlandish things on their bucket list, but when it comes to planning the goals that they live by, they play it safe. It's time to write your bucket list and let it inspire your goals!

Go back to the SWOT Around the Wheel that you did in the last chapter as you looked at each key area of your life and analyzed your Strengths, Weaknesses, Opportunities, and Threats. Take a look at the different areas of your life and consider what you wrote. What strengths can you leverage to help you tackle some of your weaknesses? Can you capitalize on a certain opportunity with the right planning? Is a specific weakness holding you back? Or is have you simply been secretly dreaming about something, and now you're ready to make it happen?

Let your imagination run away with you and create a list of goals that make you want to jump out of bed in the morning. Joe Vitale says a goal should scare you a little and excite you a lot.[22]

As you write your goals, say them out loud. Try them on for size. Picture yourself checking them off your list. The ones that you are the giddiest about are the ones you will focus on.

FOCUS TASK #9
Turn Your Bucket List into a Goals Wish List

I want you to go back to each area of your life (family, career, finances, health, spirituality, relationships, personal development, recreation, and education) and create your bucket list. This is an unfiltered, no-holds-barred-if-there-were-no-obstacles-in-your-way list.

Drop everything you've ever dreamed of in the buckets. This isn't a time to limit your ideas. Start out by listing everything that comes to mind for each area without analyzing them. Just do a brain dump and get them all out. Think about all the things you've ever wanted for each bucket. Write down everything you've ever dreamed of. Maybe you want to spend a summer in Europe or compete in a triathlon. This is the time to dream.

Once you've listed out everything, review them and put a star next to the items that excite you. We'll use these starred items as goal starters for your goal wish list in the next chapter.

FOCUS TASK #10
Create Your Vision Board

Once you've narrowed down your goals wish list to the ones that really motivate you, create a vision board representing what you want to accomplish. Have fun with it, be playful. Search for images online or off that motivate you. Get ready to see your vision and goals come to life. We start action planning soon. Once you've created your vision board, make sure you put it in a visible spot so that it can inspire you daily. (If you need guidance on creating your vision board, check out the resources in the Full-Plate Detox Group on Facebook (www.facebook. com/groups/FullPlateDetox.)

CHAPTER FIVE

Energy Expenditure and Portion Control

NOW THAT YOUR VISION board has a place of honor where you can see it daily, it's time to decide which goals you'll tackle first. You'll also have to decide what you'll take off your plate. Since we can't create more time, we have to make room by using portion control principles in order to have more of our cravings.

You'll have to put on your thinking hat and start being picky about what you put on your plate. The good news is, back in Chapter 3, you took a look at what was on your plate, and in the last chapter, you created a wish list of goals you're craving. So you know what you want to eliminate and, more importantly, what you want to obtain.

One of my best life lessons came from my son. At the age of eight, he declared that he was going to be an engineer when he grew up. He talked about it like it was a done deal. He described all the incredible things he would design to make our lives better. He created drawings and models of what he's already built in his mind. Watching him taught me the value of imagination, visualization, and believing in yourself. His commitment to this goal is a driving force in his young life. As long as he has the passion for this adventure, we feed it. He's in robotics. He watches videos about making things. He is always learning about how things work and how they fail. He is invested in his dream. That is the motivating power of visualizing your goal. I want you to have the same passion, clarity, and drive about your goals.

Let's put your planning muscles to work and start mapping out how you'll make more room on your plate. It's time to invest in your dreams. It's time to write some beautiful audacious get-you-fired-up-in-the-belly goals!

Energy Expenditure

In the first chapter, we talked about shifting your mindset from thinking you can manage or control time to focusing on where you invest your energy and time. Each day, you have twenty-four hours to invest. You should invest seven to nine of those hours in sleep. This has numerous benefits for your productivity, mental health, and overall well-being. If you completed the Time Log activity, you should also have a solid idea of how much time you are spending on different activities, such as commuting to work, social media, lost time, etc. When you are choosing where you'd rather spend your time, this activity will help you figure out what you can let go of so you can focus on what energizes you.

Deciding what to let go of won't be easy. You're committed to people. You'll probably feel guilty about cutting back on your volunteer time. You'll feel like a flake for skipping out on meetings or reducing time spent hanging out with your friends. Here's the thing: When you say "yes" to others, you are saying "no" to yourself. It might be easier to think of it as saying "not right now" to them so you can make yourself a priority today. The SWOT analysis you completed in the earlier chapter will come in handy as we start considering where you'll invest your energy and what resources you have to help you.

Let's go back to our SHEro, Brenda, who was dissatisfied with her health viewpoint. When she did her SWOT Analysis, she realized that she had more to work with than she thought. Brenda realized that she is healthy enough to exercise (Strength), but she hates working out on her own (Weakness). Luckily, she has a friend close by who wants to run a 5K with her, so she has an accountability partner if she wants one (Opportunity). The trouble is, she hates running in the cold, and winter is here (Threat). How does she stay on track? On her vision board, she has a picture of the 5K finish line. She has to figure out how to fit the time to train for the 5K in her schedule. Brenda has to determine her Opportunity cost so that she can focus her energy.

I first learned about the Opportunity cost from one of my mentors, Barbara Hemphill, a pioneer in the organizing and productivity industry.[23] I've seen this play out in many ways. Essentially, I learned that my job as a consultant wasn't to make decisions and choices for my clients. My job was simply to present them with options and help them understand how choosing one option over the other would impact them. I had to help them understand what it would cost them to choose one opportunity over another.

When you choose to do something, you're also choosing *not* to do something. You're saving your energy by not doing option A so you can better invest your energy on option B. In Brenda's case, she had to factor in how to figure out a new routine that let her train consistently with her BFF. She realized she was willing to pay the opportunity cost and give up some time on social media and sitting through HOA meetings so that she could reconnect with her friend while getting fit.

Another consideration when it comes to energy expenditure involves setting boundaries and personal policies. One of the best pieces of advice I ever received was from an early mentor, productivity expert Chris Crouch. He said these profound words. "You are what you allow."[24] Let that sink in.

If you allow other people, excuses, or distractions to deter you from your goal, they will be successful. If Brenda allows the cold weather to be a roadblock, then she won't train enough. If you allow other people to have a higher priority on your calendar, then you won't be able to work on your new goals. What will you allow?

When I started my business, family and friends assumed that they could put all my supposed extra time to good use. Suddenly, I was the go-to person to take one friend's daughter to the doctor. Another dropped in unexpectedly. Yet others called me up to chat during the day. I was equally guilty, using my work time to take care of household chores. Finally, I had to come up with personal policies and guidelines about my hours and how I would make working from home a success. I created a work schedule and let others know when I was available— and when I wasn't. I became super protective of my calendar. I created a dedicated work space and went as far as "going to work each day" by walking out the back door, around the house, and then into work through the front door. I let my friends and family know when I had scheduled breaks and down time to chill. I applied the 80/20 rule, and, to this day, have a protected time slot on my calendar that I dedicate to my most important tasks for the day.

In order to work on your goals, you'll have to set personal boundaries to minimize distractions and resist shiny new objects. Believe me, distractions will come. You will face challenges, and you'll have a ton of stuff trying to pull you back down to the bottom of your priority list if you don't have clear-cut boundaries. Brenda, for example, will have to set boundaries to protect her training time so she can make it to the finish line at her 5K.

We already know that you can't do everything at once or be everything to everyone. As you make decisions about what you want to do, consider the opportunity cost for each item you put on your plate. What does investing your time cost you, if you choose one opportunity over the other?

FOCUS TASK #11
Let It Go

As you think about all the things that drain your energy, write down what you'd like to let go of, put on the back burner, or reduce in quantity.

The amount of time you spend on social media is an easy one. In addition, consider other time wasters, such as window shopping, binge-watching shows, ironing sheets (yes, some people really do this!), cleaning everything by yourself, worrying about what you can't change, playing chauffeur to everyone else, etc.

When you are stuck, consider the opportunity cost for your energy. What could you do if you let that thing go?

Pick the Right Goals and Make them SM²ART

For this next section, you'll need your SWOT Analysis and your Goals Wish List (the list of exciting items you starred on your bucket list). We're going to use these to pick the right goals for you.

FOCUS TASK #12
Pick Three

We want to narrow down your list of Goal Starters, so you can create two or three goals to work on as you go through this detox. As you read through each Goal Starter, consider these questions when making your decision:

» Are you already working on this area? Do you already have a successful plan and system in place to achieve or fix this area? If yes, don't mess with what's in place and move on to something else.

» Do you feel thrilled and challenged to work on this area? Does it scare you a little? If yes, put a check mark and move on to the next question.

» Look at your SWOT analysis. Do you have enough working for you in the Strengths and Opportunities to offset the Weaknesses and Threats? Great, this one sounds like a winner.

»   One last question. Is it achievable? In other words, can you do it with the current skills (training/abilities) and resources (time/money) you have available today? If yes, great. Put a check mark. If you don't currently have the skills, but you're really excited about this goal, then consider setting a bridge goal to develop the skills or resources you'll need to achieve this goal.

»   Which ones will help you grow faster or see more of the results you're looking for?

»   Rate each goal on the Excitement meter on a scale of 1–10, with 10 as "This goal really excites me" and 1 as "meh, this doesn't really do it for me." From the goals that ranked 7 or higher on the Excitement meter, can you pick 3 that you just can't wait to get started on?

Now that you've refined your goals list, it's time to create your action plan.

FOCUS TASK #13
Make Your Goals SM²ART

It's time to make your goals SM²ART. SMART goals (specific, measurable, achievable, relevant, and time-bound) have been around for a long time. Most people use them at work. They are a tried-and-true way to keep you focused on your end game by stating exactly what you want to achieve and when. I'll be honest, they are usually very cut and dry and can even sound boring. So I add the extra M so you can write a SMART goal with a little *oomph* in it.

Below is my formula and definition for each stage of a SM²ART goal.

Specific: Be crystal clear and say exactly what you will accomplish when you reach your goal. Remember, you want to be able to visualize it.

Measurable: How will you know when you've completed the goal? Come up with an objective measurement. Can you quantify it in numbers, identify a tangible outcome, or establish measurable success criteria?

Motivating: Use language that excites you and pumps you up. Write your goal in a positive, empowering voice. Make it extra special and come up with a song title or tagline that captures the emotion you feel about accomplishing this goal. Make one up if you can't find one.

Achievable: What are the realistic actions that you can do right now? These actions must be matched with the existing skills and resources that you have. Don't set a goal based on a resource or skill that you don't yet have. If you have to develop a new skill or find a new resource, then you need to create a bridge goal to acquire it first and then come back to this goal.

Relevant: Remember our Funnel Vision? When you think about this goal, how does it connect to your vision? Does it pass the funnel test and support your long-term vision?

Time Bound: Set a realistic deadline for accomplishing your goal that you will meet. Give yourself enough time to meet your goal without creating unnecessary stress, but don't drag it out or procrastinate.

Words matter. When you write your goals, use inspiring language that will help you visualize the goal. Be very specific about what you'll achieve but put some swag into it.

Let's go back to Brenda's goal to train with her friend and run the 5K. Here is what this might look like as a SM^{2}ART goal:

"I will effortlessly run a sub-twenty-five-minute
5k with my BFF at the end of the summer."

Specific: She will be able to run a 5K.

Measurable: She knows the distance of the 5K and what twenty-five minutes looks like.

Motivating: "Effortlessly" means that she won't hurt while running.

Achievable: She will leverage accountability to her BFF and her time spent training.

Relevant: She wants to get back into shape to be healthy.

Time-Bound: They registered for a race at the end of the summer.

Now, to make it extra special, she added a tagline: "Girl, You Run the World." For the cherry on top, she created a play list with songs with the word "run" in the title.

Exercise Portion Control and Water the Right Habits

Before I release you into writing your goals, I want to cover a few points that can block you if you let them. While you need to evaluate your readiness to pursue your goals, you'll want to watch out for the negative self-talk and bad habits that will creep in. That's where portion control, habits, and mindset can help.

My nutritionist taught me that controlling my portions and the frequency of my meals will make the difference in my weight management success. It's not that I can't have chocolate, I just can't have as much chocolate as I used to.

When it comes to working your goals, you will have to control your energy and the amount of attention that you give to distractions. You'll have to *minimize* the amount or portion of attention that you give to distractions, bad habits, and negative self-talk. You'll have to *increase* the amount of attention that you give to your goals and the habits that support them.

Think of your goals and habits as a flowerbed. The pretty beautiful flowers are the good goals and habits that you want to cultivate. Given the right attention and nourishment (faithful practice), they will continue to flourish. From time to time, bad habits creep in like weeds. If left unattended, they will choke out the life and energy from your beautiful goals. The habits you water and give energy to are the ones that will grow.

The more you reinforce or support the habit, the deeper the roots go and the harder it is to change. Don't spend your energy worrying about a bad habit. That just helps it take deeper root. Stop watering it with attention and focus on a healthier habit instead.

In order to change, stop trying to dig out the bad habits and, instead, just plant the seeds for new habits. Give the new habits attention by reinforcing them with affirmations and positive associations with what is already working for you. You have to water the right habits and the right goals.

Early in my entrepreneur career, I realized that I had developed some bad work habits. These poor habits were not helping me as I transitioned into working on my own. I didn't realize how much time I was giving to unnecessary things. In order to walk my talk, I had to put some things on my "not-to-do" list.

I was a horrible perfectionist, and spent tons of time making things "perfect." When working on my own, I realized I wasn't producing as much as I wanted to and had to make some tough choices. I became a stickler for deadlines in my work. I committed to activities and deadlines publicly so that other people would hold me accountable.

Perfectionism is on my "not-to-do" list. I tell people that I'm a serial perfectionist in recovery and ask them to help me out. (I'm still in recovery, by the way). Instead of worrying about perfection, I focused on finishing my projects within a reasonable time. I used the mantra, "done is better than none." As my completion rate on my projects grew, I noticed the increase in productivity, income, and my emotional state. That fueled me to keep going.

One bad habit stole time from me in a sneaky way. When I worked corporate, taking a break to walk down to the cafeteria and make a cup of coffee was actually helpful. I had a chance to stretch my legs, chat with my co-worker for a minute, and grab my favorite pick-me-up.

When I worked from home, though, taking a break for coffee meant a run to my favorite coffee shop. (I thought it was a waste to brew an entire pot just for me.) Well, thirty-something minutes and five dollars later, I meandered back to my home office and tried to get back to work. It took me a while to get back into work mode. When I added up the time and money associated with that coffee run (gas and billable hours included), I had to quit the habit. I bought a single-cup brew coffee machine with a reusable filter and saved a lot of money and time.

Real talk about negative self-talk. One of my clients, Sara, is absolutely brilliant at what she does. She is a great consultant and problem-solver for her clients. She has wanted to launch her own business for so long but has talked herself out of it for years. Her negative self-talk forced her to keep working for others, minimizing her greatness, and left her stuck in neutral.

She put off her dream for years because she was full of self-doubt. Her Negative Nelly kept telling her that her skills weren't enough, that her talent wasn't enough, that she wouldn't get others to pay her for the very things her employer is paid well for now. She had to work to conquer the self-doubt and quiet Negative Nelly so she could reach for her dream.

Watch out for your negative self-talk and how it can limit your opportunities.

Mindset and Motivation Matters: Focus on Growth

I promised you that I'd tell you the truth in this book. One bit of truth that you'll have to embrace from here on out is that you will be uncomfortable as you start the work. I've worked with many a successful woman. I don't know one who never battled the feeling of not being good enough. It's a common reaction to being new at something. One thing that will help is getting comfortable with being uncomfortable. As you start changing your habits and working on your goals, you can easily focus on what you aren't good at. Don't let that stop you.

Let me introduce you to the growth mindset.

In her groundbreaking book, *Mindset: The New Psychology of Success*, Caroline S. Dweck reveals results from decades of research on success.[25] She explains how our mindset as we work on our goals can determine our success. Your mindset is your self-theory about yourself.

Many of us have been programmed with what is called a fixed mindset or the notion that we're as good as we're ever going to get. That our intelligence and capacity for growth and development has a fixed level. Someone with a fixed mindset believes that they are born with all the smarts, talent, and skills they will ever have. They believe a cap is set in place on what they can do and achieve. When we measure things in terms of "good vs. bad," we limit ourselves and our ability to succeed.

Someone with a growth mindset acknowledges areas where they can grow and believes that if they put in the effort, they can improve skills, gain knowledge, and learn new talents.

A person with a growth mindset doesn't say 'I can't do it." They say, "I can't do it *yet*." They are motivated by the notion that even if they make a mistake along the way, they are continually learning and growing and will one day achieve their goals. Instead of saying what they're bad at, they acknowledge it but leave room for growth. Brenda went from saying, "I can't even run five minutes" to "I will get strong enough to run a whole 5K."

This mindset fosters the desire to push through when things get tough. The right mindset is the difference between waking up before dawn to pound the pavement and lazing around the house all day. Some folks think if they just write down their goals, try their best, and visualize success, they will succeed. In fact, these are the three biggest myths about motivation that won't go away, according to Heidi Grant Halvorson PhD, author of *The Science of Success*.[26]

FOCUS TASK #14
Mindset Matters, Water the Right Habit

Start thinking about the habits you want to cultivate to support your goals. If a thought about a bad habit kicks in, flip it by writing a positive new habit to replace it. Come up with growth mindset mantras to help you water the right habits.

Jump Some Hurdles

Writing down your goals and visualizing success is only part of the formula. You'll have to picture yourself jumping hurdles. This means you may have to visualize not just reaching your goal, but imaging yourself meeting and overcoming obstacles along the way. It helps to come up with sayings or mantras to say when you encounter these obstacles. That's like Brenda's tagline "Girl, you run the world."

As you write your goals and think of your skills, remember, you can't do it yet, but you're going to!

FOCUS TASK #15
Jumping Hurdles

We want to set you up for success. As you are writing your goals, you may need to mentally work past the obstacles in order to clear your path if you are having trouble picturing your outcome. This activity will be helpful for you to look for possible hurdles you'll have to jump to reach your goals. Answer these questions for each goal:

>> What will my completed goal actually look like?
>> What will be the final outcome?
>> What will a day in my life feel like once I've hit this goal?
>> What would failure look like?
>> What's the worst thing that could happen as I work towards this goal?
>> What can I do to avoid a negative outcome?
>> What are am I allowing or tolerating that might impact this goal?
>> Where do I need to set boundaries to make sure I don't steal time from my goals?
>> What do I have to stop, minimize, keep doing, do more of or start doing in order to reach this goal?

Get Ready to Move from Vision to Action

A quote that really centered my thinking on vision and goal setting is by Joel Barker:

> "Vision without action is just a dream.
> Action without vision is just passing the time.
> Vision with action can change the world."[27]

If you only focus on your vision, then you'll spend your time dreaming. If you run around busy without purpose, you are confusing activity with accomplishment. When you plug your daily actions into your vision, you can and will change your world. Get ready to move from vision to action!

I know you are anxious to get to the doing, but this work to dive deep into your goal and the game plan we're going to create in the next chapter will make the rest of what we do so much easier.

49

I want you to realize that you have done a ton of heavy lifting by analyzing what's working, deciding what you want to eliminate, acknowledging goal blocking behaviors, and creating a list of what you're craving. Keep up the amazing work. This will pay off in the end.

CHAPTER SIX

Creating Your Healthy Plate

FOR INFORMATION JUNKIES, gathering details and planning can be a favorite past time. For others, taking the time to plan is a painful process. If you fall into the first category, get ready to have some fun. If you fall into the second group, while you may be chomping at the bit and ready to jump right into working on your goals, you have one important thing to do before you dive right in. You need to create your game plan.

When I was in high school, several friends were in the Marine Corp Cadets. They walked around singing cadences and quoting their ROTC drill sergeants. One friend had a favorite saying about planning. (I'm giving you the edited version here.) *Proper Planning* Prevents Poor Performance. *Hoorah!*[28]

Planning advocates will sing the praises of planning. Antoine de Saint-Exupéry said, "a goal without a plan is just a wish."[29] A common proverb tells us that "if you fail to prepare you are preparing to fail."[30, 31] One more favorite quote follows: "Plans are worthless, but planning is everything."[32, 33] If all these greats found planning to be so awesome, why do people run from it?

The answer can be found in this familiar Yiddish proverb. "Man plans, and God laughs" or in the Allen Saunders quote that "life is what happens to you while you're busy making other plans."[34]

Even with the best plans, something can and probably will go wrong. Life does not necessarily happen the way you pictured it. Don't let that scare you away from creating a plan to reach your goals. Although your plan might not work out exactly the way you planned it, you're still more likely to achieve your goal. Your journey there might just look differently than you thought.

Planning is one of the most important steps toward goal achievement. Without it, you might continue on the same path of being overwhelmed, overloaded, and stuck with a lot of junk on your plate.

Coming up with the idea is easy. Picturing the finish line is motivating. Planning how you will get there can be tedious and not as much fun—but you can't skip this step. If you fail to plan, you plan to fail.

You will stretch your planning muscles and really think about how you're going to work your goals. Think of this as designing the ideal menu for your healthier plate.

Puzzle Pieces

If you haven't figured it out, I geek out about planning. It was one of the things that initially drew me to my first career in advertising. We researched, conducted focus groups, wrote reports, and made recommendations. The best part was when we turned all that work and strategy into awesome commercials. I loved watching the process go from a simple concept to a storyboard to rough cuts (the first version of a commercial), and then to the finished product on TV. I loved watching the final result. In order to move through the process, we had teams that each played their role. We knew that each department was just part of the process and pieces of the puzzle.

To me, planning is like putting together the pieces of a puzzle. I have a lot of respect for anyone who can complete a puzzle without a picture as a reference. I have even more admiration for those who can start with random pieces and complete the puzzle. My personal strategy is to look for the corner pieces and build the puzzle from the outside in. Once I have a sense of the frame, it's easier to fill in the rest of the puzzle.

When it comes to reaching your goals, there is a strategic component to planning how you will achieve them. You have to find those "corner pieces" to build the framework of your game plan.

The Strategy Behind Your Plan

Plan backward. When you set a SM²ART goal, you have a deadline. When you plan backward, you start with the end in mind. Think about the last thing you need to check off your list to hit your goal. Write it down. Then ask yourself, what happens right before that and write that down. Keep working your way backward, asking the same question. "What needs to happen right before this step?"

As you plan, think about how long you need for each phase so that you can schedule accordingly. Will you be on vacation? Will you have a big project due? Will the kids be home for a school break? Try to avoid having deadlines that conflict with other scheduled items that you won't be able to change.

Try not to drag things out longer than they need to be, but don't procrastinate either. Parkinson's Law can kick in and create havoc in your schedule. Parkinson's Law is the idea that "work expands to fill the time available for its completion." If you have three months to do something, you can either stretch the work out to fill three months, or you can fit three months of work into three weeks if you're a procrastinator. Make sure your deadlines are realistic.

Shorten your time frame. Looking too far down the road might set you up for failure. We live in a world of instant gratification. We have been programmed to do everything as quickly as we can. While you may be working on a big, long-term goal, looking at a finish line that's years down the road can be defeating. Breaking down your plan into short-term goals will increase your success rate. It's easier to picture finishing something three to four months down the road than a year in the future. Set milestones for your plan that give you immediate wins to leverage along the way.

Plan the forest and count the trees. You have to be able to see both the forest and the trees. Some of us find it easy to come up with a big beautiful plan but find it hard to wrangle all the details. Some of us are great at logistics and details but forget to pick up our heads up to see the bigger picture. In order for your plan to be successful, you have to do both. Keep your eye on the prize while making sure all the parts keep moving in sync.

Divide up your plate. Think of your entire plate. What percentage is already committed to things you *must* do, such as work, sleep, and commuting? How much of your plate does that leave, and what's the best way to divide that time? Portion-control your time. My nutritionist had me target a mix of 50 percent carbs, 25 percent fat, and 25 percent protein. This helps me maintain a balanced plate. So if 60 percent of your time is split between the *must-dos*, then how can you split the remaining 40 percent so that you can focus on your goals?

Put on the right thinking hat. Edward de Bono is well known in the field of creative thinking; in fact, he originated the concept of lateral thinking, which is about taking an indirect and creative approach to problem solving and thinking out of the box. Edward de Bono is particularly well-known for his development of the Six Thinking Hats.[35] When you wear the right hat at different phases of planning, you will be sure to consider the problem from all the right angles. Here are the six hats:

1. When you wear the **white** hat, you remain neutral and objective while you consider the facts and information available to you. Your goal here is to fill in the information gaps. What details do you have about your goal? How long will it take you? What

resources do you need? What obstacles do you have to overcome to achieve your goal? Stick to the facts and just the facts.

2. Under the **red** hat, you get to express all your emotions, feelings, intuition, and hunches. You don't have to worry about being rational or making sense. You just get to consider your likes, dislikes, fears, what you love, and even what you hate about the situation. With the red hat, it's *all* about the feels!

3. The **black** hat will probably feel the most comfortable. The black hat brings Negative Nelly into the conversation as she identifies everything that can go wrong with the plan. While the black hat is important, it can also be overused because we fall into judgment and criticism so easily. Wear it with caution.

4. You guessed it, **yellow** is for sunshine, optimism, brightness, and positive thinking. Wearing this hat means you look for the silver lining in the cloud. This is the glass-is-half-full—and there's another jug of plenty—mindset. Look for the benefit and upside. For example, what are the possibilities once you reach your goal? What else will you be able to do? How much better will things be when you're finished? Everything is awesome- you just have to see it.

5. **Green** is for growth, creativity, and new ideas. When you wear the green hat, you focus on alternative ideas and on ways to solve your problem. You seek and bring in new perspectives. You let your imagination fly to find out-of-the-box ideas. Don't fall back to the same old, same old. Break the mold and throw out your old way of approaching problems. Get rid of the thought "I always do it this way" and try something new.

6. Finally, the **blue** hat is used to manage the thinking process. Ideally, you put it on at the start of the process to organize how you will tackle the problem. The blue hat is about the process. Think of it as the conductor of the orchestra or as the project manager. You can use the blue hat to summarize your thinking and create your sequence for how you'll tackle your situation.

When I wanted to write a book, I had to put my thinking hats on. It went a little something like this:

» **Blue hat**: How will I write this book? Do I know where to start? I decided to join a writer's boot camp and give myself over to an expert to coach me through the process.

» **Red hat**: I was nervous about writing a book. I was excited to finally convey my process in writing. I felt proud and ready to tell my story after my years in business. I was scared about writing the book and managing the creative process. I was frustrated when I was writing the book and the words weren't flowing the way I wanted them to. It was fun writing this book. I was jumping for joy when I finally finished my manuscript.

» **White hat**: What statistics, research, strategies did I want to include? What client stories did I want to share? What personal stories did I think were relevant? What resources or ideas would improve this book?

» **Black hat**: Negative Nelly was busy. Why would anyone want to read this book? What if no one is interested? What makes my approach so unique or different? What am I committing to? What if I invest in the boot camp and can't see it through? What if I get writer's block when I'm on a tight deadline? What if the material is no good? (I could go on here!)

» **Yellow hat**: Wow, this book will finally allow me to broaden my message and share my insights with more than my private clients. I know my process works and writing this book will give me a platform from which I can launch speaking and coaching engagements. This book will share a proven process that will help many people. People will like the book and the process I share.

» **Green hat**: Coming up with the concept of the full-plate detox was a unique way of framing the conversation of how we invest our time and energy. It allows me to play on the idea of diet and detox and explain our use of time in a context people can understand.

How can this process help you plan your goals?

Create an annual goal, but act on it quarterly. I've been doing this kind of planning for years because it keeps my eyes on the bigger picture, but I only have to tackle what's in front of me. You start out with a bigger goal and then break it down into manageable time frames. This is great if you are working on something that will take you a long time to achieve. You just have to focus on the tasks and milestones that are coming up soon. If we schedule our goals and focus on setting quarterly goals that keep us on the path to our bigger objectives, we're more likely to succeed.

In his book, *The Twelve-Week Year,* Brian Moran teaches this concept by recommending we plan our goals in twelve-week time periods.[36] You approach reaching your goal in twelve weeks with the same energy and focus you do at the end of the calendar year when you try to hit your goals.

Start out by creating an annual goal (it doesn't matter what month you're in). You then break that goal down into quarterly objectives, identifying key accomplishments that you'll need to hit to stay on track. Then take those quarterly objectives and break them down into monthly milestones. Figure out what progress you need to make on a monthly basis to stay on track with your quarterly goals. Monthly milestones are then translated into weekly work. By this point, you should be scheduling commitments on your calendar. Try to plan a few weeks out so you have room to adjust if things come up. Weekly work becomes daily tasks that are booked as appointments on your calendar.

Have a plan behind your plan. Since we know the reality check is out there just waiting to throw a monkey wrench in your best laid plans, you have to be prepared. I believe in contingency and back-up plans, the plans behind the plan.

To be successful in today's ever-changing world, you have to be flexible and agile by preparing for possible scenarios. You can't be too attached to your plan because you'll freak out if it fails. As you organize your plan, consider the hurdles or obstacles you might encounter as you are planning. Think of a few options in case problems arise and move on. Just don't become a forever planner who becomes so stuck in trying to plan for every contingency that you're caught in analysis paralysis.

Guess what? Now it's time to build your game plan!

FOCUS TASK #16
Create your Goal-Getter Action Plan

Planning Tip:

I like to use a mind map to plan out my goals and projects. (If you're not familiar with mind maps, check out the Resources tab in the Detoxers group).

Take each one of your SM^{2}ART goals and put them through your process. Start with your due date and plan backward to lay out the actions and milestones you'll need to check off in order to reach your goal. Identify the different things you'll have to do to accomplish your goals. Put on the six thinking hats for each goal so you can plan for obstacles, explore new ideas, and give space for your feelings and other influences.

Happy planning!

CHAPTER SEVEN

Cleansing Your Calendar

LET THE CALENDAR CLEANSING begin! If you have never done a detox, you usually need to prepare a bit or get ready to ease you into things.

The good news is that you have already done your prep for the full-plate detox. We are going to start putting your plan of action into place—*finally*! We just have to make sure you have the space on your calendar for what you're really craving, so it's time to start the detox and get rid of the junk. It's like Thanksgiving dinner. When the table and your plate is full, the only way you can fit everything in is to eat in waves. (Or am I the only one that grazes all day?)

Basically, your body needs a break to digest the food you've already eaten to make room for more goodies. In this chapter, we need to make room on your schedule by aligning your calendar with your plate— taking the wrong things off your calendar and filling it back up with the right things.

As you make changes to your calendar, you will take the time to find the right mix. Try out things. Make adjustments. Tweak things. Make it work for you.

Cleanse and Purge

A few years ago, I had to make a few difficult decisions about my calendar. I had been serving on non-profit boards and other volunteer groups for over ten years. I love giving back and getting involved with my community. When I relocated, I continued that practice. But I encountered a scheduling problem when my work schedule started picking up as I established my business in my new home. Some aggravating factors, such as increased time on the road and shifts in my daily routine, made it hard to fit commitments in the way I used to. As life became busier, I struggled more to juggle everything on my calendar. I had to make tough choices to cut back on some of my volunteer roles. I still support my community, but I now do so in ways that don't add additional burdens to my schedule.

In order to adjust, I had to ditch the automatic yes. My desire to help others often led me to say "yes" whenever someone asked me to help out, sit on a committee, or volunteer my time or services. The automatic yes can often lead to calendars that are filled with activities that aren't really important or connected to your goals.

You may have a hard time with the automatic yes. In fact, you might even suffer from what I call "volunteer-itis," where you actually jump in and offer your services, even if no one asks you to. You might be your own worst enemy. Recognize that you have the right to say no. When you say "yes" to someone else, you're saying "no" to your own priorities. Don't prioritize someone else above yourself.

Keep a clear picture of what really matters to you so that you can say no to what will distract you. Schedule your personal priorities on your calendar as "appointments with yourself." If you already have a full schedule, be sure to eliminate one task before you take on another. Practice saying "no" to gain confidence and to learn how to feel comfortable while doing so. (Seriously, look at yourself in the mirror and practice saying "no.") Never postpone your own plans to please someone else simply because they can be postponed. Only commit to something after you have considered the importance of your own plans vs. the new request.

As you get ready to cleanse and purge your calendar, you'll have to go through each activity and cancel or drop whatever is not in alignment with your goals. You can't do it all—at least not at once. Cleansing your calendar means making tough decisions about what you'll do when.

I have watched the movie *Girls Trip (2017)* a few times, which has a lot of laughs and truths that hit home. The movie also includes some heart-piercing moments when the friends were talking about the different choices they made. Regina Hall's character, Ryan Pierce, was a motivational speaker who told women that "they could have it all."[37] This mindset isn't a bad thing, in and of itself. My question is, "Does it have to be all at once?" Trying to do everything all at once is keeping you *off balance and off purpose.*

As an entrepreneur, one of the hardest lessons I learned was that just because I *could* do anything I want, I didn't *have* to. I fell into the trap of becoming excited each time I saw a new program, class, or service that other consultants were doing that I knew I could pull off. I would drop what I was working on and then jump into the new, next best, latest-and-greatest thing. Eventually, I had a trail of half-finished projects and nothing productive or completed to show for my time. And I wasn't alone. Many of my entrepreneur clients have struggled with this same issue. I teach them what I had to learn the hard way—become very picky about what you invest your time in and focus only on what will help you reach your goal.

I've talked about the importance of making choices and that in and of itself, not choosing is a choice. William James said it this way: **"When you have to make a choice and don't make it, that is in itself a choice."**[38] You can continue down the same path and look back a year from now and wonder why nothing has changed, *or* you can choose to change. You can choose where you invest your time. It's time to choose. Cleansing your calendar is about choosing to make changes *now* so that a year from now, you don't regret a thing. Carl Sandberg says, "Time is the coin of your life. It is the only coin you have, and only you can determine how it will be spent."[39] Let's make some wise choices!

It's About Habits, Not Apps

As a productivity coach and trainer, I am often asked which are the best options for calendars, tools, or apps. It's easy to get caught up in the notion that a tool or application will be the magic pill that you're looking for to change the way you're working. I have seen people become excited about a system or a tool that works for a friend, and then feel defeated and disappointed when the same system doesn't work for them.

Here's the deal: there is no cookie-cutter solution or a one-size-fits-all approach. What works for one person may or may not work for another. And no matter how good the application or tool, it will only work as well as your habits.

In his book, *The Power of Habit: Why We Do What We Do in Life and Business*, Carl Duhigg talks about how we form habits through what he calls the habit loop. The habit loop is kicked off by the cue that signals the brain to start a specific routine that you do once the cue happens with the goal of reaching the reward or pay-off for completing the routine. In order to make changes to our behaviors, we have to unpack our habit loop and figure out what we can change to turn a negative habit into a positive one. If you make a change in the habit loop, you'll change the habit—or better yet, start a new one. Duhigg recommends examining the habit loop and experimenting with changes to either the cue, routine, or reward to instill healthier habits.[40]

Let's say you want to start going back to the gym. Think about your typical routine. What keeps you from going to the gym? Are your gym clothes ready when you drive by the gym, or did you leave them at home? Are you too tired at the end or the start of the day? Is the gym thirty minutes in the other direction? Change something.

Try putting your gym clothes in the car or keep a set at work to eliminate that excuse. Try switching the time of day you go to the gym. Put the gym class on your schedule. Set an alarm. Find a gym buddy who will meet you at class. Switch to a closer gym. If you've already done those things, consider changing the reward. Set a target of going to the gym three times a week and reward yourself with a night out with friends at the end of the month if you hit your goal three out of four weeks. Change something!

Take note of the bad habits that often stop your progress. Perfectionism, procrastination, and multi-tasking will all block your goals. Watch out for how they show up and break the habit loop by changing something in your routine.

Eat Your Frogs

Though the sentiment is credited to Mark Twain, it was Nicholas Chamfort who said, "Eat a live frog[41] every morning, and nothing worse will happen to you the rest of the day."[42] The "live frog" that he's referring to is that project that you've been dreading and putting off for a long time. If you get in the habit of tackling that tough project first thing in your day, you won't be worried about it all day long. This quote inspired Brian Tracey's book, *Eat That Frog!* in which he shares time-management strategies focused on helping you prioritize your work.[43]

You might cringe at the thought of tackling that tough project in the morning, but Nicholas was onto something. I was resistant to the idea at first. I am a night owl by nature. I used to stay up under the bedsheets with a flashlight reading as a kid. I tend to get my second and third wind at night and can power through hours of work in the wee hours of the morning. Looking back, I developed this habit from years of fielding client phone calls and meetings during the day. I could then work at night when the ringing stopped.

Being a night owl is okay every once in a while, but the constant late hours will have a negative impact. Without the science lesson, your cortisol levels rise when you don't get enough sleep. Cortisol is a hormone linked to weight gain and stress levels. In addition to promoting weight gain, I struggled to pry my eyes open when I had to get up, take care of my son, and follow up with my clients the next day.

Despite my initial skepticism, I learned that by eating that frog in the morning, I had a less stressful day and was better prepared to handle emergencies and fires when they cropped up. I block off the first two hours of each day for my frog/focus work and protect that time fiercely. I only give up that time for paid client opportunities or for necessary tasks that cannot be moved to another time.

Try eating a frog. Think about a project or task that you typically put off. Schedule time on your calendar in the morning and commit to making headway on that project. When you eat the frog early in the day, that project won't hang over your head like a prison sentence. You can still work your circadian rhythm if you tend to peak later in the day by dedicating that second burst of energy to problem-solving or creative work. As you start cleansing your calendar, try to figure out your best time for focus work, problem-solving, research, meetings, or being creative, and set aside time on your calendar for those.

Calendaring Best Practices

If you don't actually use a calendar, we're going to start there. Trying to make it through your crazy busy life without a calendar is like trying to carry a gallon of water in your bare hands. It won't work. Things will slip through the cracks.

Our brains can only keep track of so many activities, appointments, and deadlines, so we need a place to park that running task list and set aside time for project work.

To make this work, you'll need a calendar.

Paper or Electronic?

Some folks are partial to paper, and I'm not knocking that. However, I strongly recommend using an electronic calendar. Here are a few reasons why:

1. First, you can always convert your calendar to paper by printing it out if you need to physically handle it. For people who process kinesthetically, this is important.

2. In this modern age, so many tools and resources can be linked to an electronic calendar to make managing and sharing information easier.

3. You can design and coordinate your calendar by using color to tell a story and see where your time is invested. For example, use green for personal time, blue for work, red for critical tasks, etc.

4. You can process tasks separately from appointments without juggling lists. Both Outlook and Google have a separate task list function that makes this easier.

5. You can leverage reminders, alerts, and alarms to prompt you about your schedule instead of having to remember to check the piece of paper. Paper doesn't jump up and say, "Hey, you have a meeting." (When I worked at a corporate job, this was a huge stumbling block for me. I got so caught up in my work that I was late to meetings because the paper calendar didn't have alerts!)

If you have a smartphone, you already have access to an electronic calendar at your fingertips. Go ahead and give it a try!

Create Your Ideal Week

What does your ideal day or week look like? That's the picture you need to have in mind when you start working with your calendar. It might be easier to have themes or time blocks so you can create routines but leave room for flexibility. Time block your calendar, and create routines for doing repetitive work. When you time block, you protect key windows on your calendar as appointments.

Create time blocks for key things like checking email, project work, and working out. Be sure to leave space for a just-for-me zone. You'll want to fill up this space later with guilt-free and pleasurable activities that feed your soul. Time block options could be:

Frog or focus time: for that big project or your goal work

Admin time: for bill payment, filing, paperwork management, etc.

Family time: dinner, game time, etc.

Health: for working out, meal planning, doctor's appointments

Personal Development: skill building, schoolwork, reading, etc.

As a solopreneur, I found it useful to establish themes for my days when I was starting out: Marketing Mondays, Teaching Tuesday, Website Wednesdays, Task-List Thursdays, Follow-Up Fridays. If I didn't have something client-related booked on my calendar, I would fall back to the day's theme and tackle whatever projects I had in that area.

When you're planning your ideal day, try not to cram everything in on one day. Be sure to create appointments on your calendar for your most important project of the week. If you practice the 80/20 rule, you can create recurring time blocks on your calendar so you'll always have that space.

Remember, when you're applying the 80/20 rule, your goal is to set aside about ninety minutes, ideally three days per week, to focus on your goals and project work. This can be a single ninety-minute block of time, two forty-five-minute windows or three thirty-minute windows (nothing shorter than thirty minutes). Finally, don't allow anything on your calendar that doesn't help you reach your goals, isn't tied to your passion, or that doesn't support your vision.

Don't chase Shiny New Objects. We can play with so many beautiful shiny new things instead of working on that goal that scares us. Don't give in to what I call SNOS: Shiny New Object Syndrome.

Don't let distractions get in the way of working on your goals. If you have a great idea for something that you'd like to do, but it's not a current goal that you're working on, create a Someday/Maybe list for those things that look exciting but would pull you off a current project. Once you check items off your list, you can revisit this list to see if an idea there can pass the funnel-vision test.

I park fresh ideas on the Someday/Maybe list, especially when I'm scanning the competitive landscape (peeping at what other people are doing). If I'm so inspired, I may take time to flesh out the idea a bit, but unless it's an *amazing income-producing-now* idea, I put it on the Someday/Maybe list and consider it when I'm setting goals again.

Build in buffers: If you notice that you are always running from one meeting to the next, add some buffers to your calendar to avoid calendar traffic jams. Think of it like the bumper guards for the kids at the bowling alley. You need something between you and the next meeting. Blocking a fifteen-minute window as an appointment on your calendar at work will prevent others from booking you in back-to-back meetings. Put your lunch time on your calendar. Schedule your travel time whether you're walking or driving. Create space between meetings so you have time to gather your thoughts, grab a snack, or just walk down the hallway like a sane person.

Reference your Not-to-Do List for what you want to take off your schedule. Pull it out, and if you need to decline appointments, step off boards, or ditch the late afternoon coffee run, do it!

FOCUS TASK #17
Calendar Cleanse

Create your ideal schedule for the next two weeks. If your biggest pain points are happening at work, then start with your work calendar. Use the checklist below as you create your new schedule.

Your Calendar Cleanse Checklist

- » Get your paper or electronic calendar ready.
- » Add reminders, appointments, and tasks for your key milestones and work from your Goal-Getter Action Plan.
- » Have your Not-to-Do List handy.
- » Time block your Focus time (80/20) rule to eat that frog.
- » Create appointment buffers.
- » Color-code your important tasks.
- » Schedule energy breaks (five-minute meditation window, fifteen-minute walk, thirty-minute workout).
- » Create a playlist loaded with inspiring music for boring tasks.

CHAPTER EIGHT

Supplements and Guilt-Free Pleasures

AT SOME POINT, YOU have to take action. The great Bruce Lee said, "If you spend too much time thinking about a thing, you'll never get it done."[44]

You've dreamed. You've pruned your habits. You've done the deep reflection about your mindset. You have mapped out a plan. Now, it's time for some action!

Once you've created your schedule, you have to start living it—starting today. Take notes of what worked and what didn't work.

Think about the last line from Joel Barker's quote. "Vision with action can change the world."[45] It's time to change your world.

As you take action and make changes, you may need to adjust your plan. That's okay. It's also okay to celebrate the wins while you smooth out the process. I also want to make sure that you have the right systems in place to support you as you make these changes. Planning is great, but it's time to start doing. Adjust your time blocks as you go. Your goal is to work and tweak your new schedule until it feels right.

Start living your plan one day at a time. If you slip up, you can always get back on track tomorrow. The key is to not give up on your plan too soon.

Walt Disney said, "If you dream it you can do it!"[46] You can do this!

Supplement Your Motivation

When you start a detox for your body, health experts often recommend that you take supplements to help fill in nutrition and calorie gaps. As you go through TFPD, you'll need to supplement your motivation as you change your habits so you can see this thing through.

Our brains are lazy and crave routines and habits. The more attention you give your new daily routines by intentionally focusing on them, writing them down, and sharing them with others, the more likely you are to stick with them. Remember your vision board? Make sure you still keep it front and center.

Changing your habits and trying to do things differently will feel very strange at first. Remember, you are making your dream a reality. Don't lose sight of your dreams, vision, and goals. They may seem too big and far away right now, but you can get there one step at a time. Don't give up.

Pull out the motivation mantras that you wrote in Chapter 5 and keep them around you on post-it notes, whiteboards, three-by-five notecards, etc. These mantras will come in handy to supplement your motivation when you hit a stumbling block.

Here are some of the mantras that help supplement me when I'm starting new habits:

» A river cuts through a rock, not because of its power, but its persistence. –(Jim Watkins)[47]
» Procrastination is the thief of time. –(Edward Young)[48]
» Success is no accident. It is hard work, perseverance, learning, studying, sacrifice, and most of all, love of what you are doing or learning to do. –(Pele)[49]
» Failure is simply the opportunity to begin again, this time more intelligently. –(Henry Ford)[50]
» It always seems impossible until it's done. –(Nelson Mandela)[51]

Rally Your Cheerleaders

Having the right people in your corner as you make these changes will make your journey easier. Buddy up and gather your cheerleaders and accountability partners who will pitch in to keep you on track. A healthy support system is made up of folks that can guide, motivate, and encourage you, similar to a personal trainer for weight management or a financial planner for your finances. Depending on your goals, you might need different cheerleaders or accountability partners.

Start with your inner circle. The changes that you are making will impact them. Talk to them about what you're making room for in your life. Share why it's important to you to make these changes. Tell them about your vision. Let them know what motivates you and what stresses you out.

Talk about the goals that you've set and what reaching them will allow you to do differently—both for yourself and for them. Let them know where they fit in on your priority list.

Be mindful that as they see you make changes, canceling plans, and saying "no" more often, they may think this is a "selfish phase." By talking about your needs, goals, and motivation, you will help strengthen your commitment and teach others, especially children, about the importance of self-care. Self-care is not selfish. Taking time to develop and build your energy stores will refill that empty cup so you can give from your overflow.

Let your loved ones know that you need their support and understanding so that you can be a healthier, better version of yourself. The more you take care of yourself, the more you can help them.

Hopefully, your family will get on board. In case they aren't the right ones to support you in your goals, carefully pick the right cheerleaders. My mom used to tell me that people will "know me by the company I keep." As I've grown older, this saying has even deeper meaning. You will only do as well as the people you surround yourself with.

Stick with like-minded people with positive growth mindsets

who also believe in doing the necessary work to reach their goals. Maybe you have a friend who is struggling with the same challenge. As accountability partners, you can check in with each other, strategize, lift one another's spirits, help each other stay on track, and celebrate the wins.

Consider pulling in a few respected peers as your advisory board. Use them as brainstorming partners, mastermind conspirators, and the best cheerleading squad a girl could have.

If you don't have anyone to believe in you, you have to believe in yourself. But hopefully, you have someone in your corner to share this journey with. Leverage our Full-Plate Detox social media group and local networking opportunities to start connecting with goal-oriented peers.

When all else fails, reach out to me in the Detoxers' group, and we'll connect you with the right support.

When You Need an Energy Boost

I won't sugarcoat this process and act like everything will always be sunshine and roses. From time to time, you may need an energy boost if you're struggling to stick to your plan or if you face challenges. Learn to recalibrate.

You will hit stumbling blocks. Plan for them. Don't give up just because you miss a deadline or something didn't go according to plan. Stay the course. When situations come up that you didn't plan for, evaluate how to adjust and fit in these interruptions.

Try the Four *R*s of Goal-Getting to get back on track:

1. **Regroup**: Gather the troops. Go back to your sounding board and pull together your advisory board. Take a short break before tackling the plan again. Sometimes the plan is right, but the timing is wrong. Pressing pause might give you the space, time, or energy you need to be successful.

2. **Reframe**: Try a different perspective. The glass isn't half empty; it's half full. Heck, there's more water out there, go get more. How can you look at the problem differently? Approach the plan from a different angle by putting on your thinking hats again. Shifting your thinking may take you down a different road, but will the journey be easier. You won't know until you try.

3. **Retreat**: Fall back. Stop advancing and gather your resources. When things start to go south, sometimes you have to pull back before committing more time or resources to a sinking ship. Don't force yourself to try and see things through if all the signs point to the plan not working out. Failing is practice for getting it right. Don't be afraid to walk away from a plan that won't get you to your objective.

4. **Re-plan**: You've tried regrouping. You've reframed your thinking, and now it's time to retreat. It's not time to quit. Remember Thomas Edison and his one-thousand-step process to invent the light bulb.[52] Sometimes not succeeding is a just a step in your plan

Guilt-Free Pleasures Make the Process Easier

Guilt-free pleasures are things that you do for yourself. Consider them your rewards for achieving your goals. They are the rewards that we plan for ourselves to celebrate accomplishments and to keep us motivated as we work on our goals. They are the pay off for all our hard work.

We are used to talking about guilty pleasures, but there's no need to associate guilt with what you enjoy. Self-care, personal enjoyment, investing in your own development, and doing things for fun are all reasonable expectations of a healthy adult life. Somewhere along the way, we've been programmed to believe that fun has to stop once we reach adulthood. We make "adulting" harder than it has to be. It's healthy to enjoy guilt-free pleasures as a part of your life. In fact, it makes the hard work worth it.

I posted a question on social media, asking folks what they would do if they had more time. While a few wanted to travel more, the wish list was simple: time to craft, dance, read fiction books, cook, go to the movies, play games, hike, sleep, or watch reality TV. Our wishes aren't excessive. So why don't we fit more in?

As a kid, I loved singing along with the song from *Mary Poppins*, "Just a Spoonful of Sugar."[53] We need more sugar in our adult lives to help make the medicine—the difficult tasks—easier to swallow. Plan some amazing rewards for yourself for hitting your goals. Mix it up. Do small things like a mini spa day, massages, your favorite dessert treats, or a paint-and-sip night. Put some big rewards on the calendar, such as a trip or a shopping spree, etc.

When I was working on my coaching certification, I spent a lot of time in class and on practical application. I needed to put in the work to reach my goal and, in doing so, had to seriously adjust my schedule.

As a thank you to my son for his patience and as a reward for completing my certification, I took my son with me to San Diego. For a week and a half, we spent time together, visiting loved ones and taking in the sights. That was one of our favorite times together. Each year, I set a big stretch goal, and I plan an appropriate reward for hitting it. What rewards will you set for rocking your goals?

Live Your Dream

My big dream goal is to be able to take summers off without worrying about income. While I was in college, I worked part-time for the New York City Department of Education. I had wonderful hours (a maximum of twenty hours a week from Monday to Friday between 7:00 a.m. and 3:00 p.m.), paid vacations, and holidays. The best part was having the entire summer off. My first corporate job was a shock to the system: twelve-hour work days, only fifteen paid holidays, and forget about taking two weeks off, much less the entire summer.

I decided that one day, I would be able to take the summer off without having to work or worry about income. I'm getting closer and closer to reaching that goal. The solopreneur life can be challenging, and believe me, I have thought about quitting at times. But then I think of my dream goal. I say, "Nicole, you're working toward summers off." In the meantime, I do my best to live out that dream in small ways.

I am super selective about the work I do in the summertime. I instituted a Fridays-off policy during the summer in my business from day #1. More recently, I have gone to a half-day policy during the week. I'm very intentional about the work that I do and still accomplish a lot, but I clear as much time as possible to make memories with my son.

While you are working on your goal, this dream might seem far in the distance. Try to incorporate aspects of that goal in your present life to keep that hope alive!

Celebrate Your Wins

It's easy to get caught up in looking for big shifts in our lives and overlook the small moments. When working with my coaching clients, I've noticed that the big shifts happen step-by-step over time. It's important to take note of the small wins and celebrate the stepping stones on your way to success. The *small victories will take you to the next level.*

Tara, a coaching client, shared that she doesn't take the time to celebrate all her successes. She'd been working really hard to overcome some obstacles, and while she could see progress, she was more focused on the big win down the road. A conversation with her daughter made her notice that she tends to skip right over all the little moments. She realized that she was teaching her daughter to just keep pushing from one goal to the next without celebrating her successes or gaining insight along the way.

Enjoy the journey. Yes, we want to hit our goals and timelines. I'm all for it. Just don't forget to stop and smell the roses and enjoy the journey along the way.

PARTING THOUGHTS

Moving from Detox to Lifestyle–Making it Last

YOU CAN'T SEE ME, but I'm doing a happy dance for you. Doing the work and making it this far is a *big deal*!

I promise to keep this chapter short and sweet. It is meant to be a bridge to help you transition from the full-plate detox into a lifestyle change.

When I sat down to write this book, I considered ending it with the previous chapter. But I realized that would not be enough. My passion is not just to help you solve a short-term problem but to help you make lasting changes in your life. I wanted to give you resources that you can use again and again to be as productive as possible so you can have more of what you crave in your life.

Now that you've come to this part of the journey, I want to leave you with a few parting thoughts to help make all these new habits stick as you shift from detox to a lifestyle.

Do Your Vision Check-Ups

True story: I almost kissed another guy on my honeymoon.

Yup. Some guy almost got lucky right in front of my newly minted husband because I couldn't see who I was swimming up to.

I have struggled with poor vision for most of my life. As a child, I had thick ugly glasses. As a teen, my father bought me contacts, but I had to give them up because my allergies and the dust from the gymnastic chalk made my eyes too dry. I went back to glasses and learned to live with them. (The first time my husband told me he loved me, he said, "I love you and your glasses.")

Around the time we married, I was trying soft contacts, but I couldn't wear them in the pool. Our first full day on our honeymoon, we went to the pool, so I took out the contacts. There I was, swimming up to my "husband" to celebrate making it through the wedding drama. As I reached out to plant a big kiss on him, someone grabbed my hand and pulled me aside. When I looked over, ready to fight, I was staring at my husband. When I looked back at the guy I had almost kissed, I realized how big a mistake I almost made! The poor guy thought he would get lucky. Whew! That was a near miss.

Thankfully, the rest of the honeymoon went off without a hitch, but you'd better believe when I came home, I promptly looked into LASIK surgery. Once I did it, I was amazed at what a difference lens-free vision was like.

The freedom to see clearly without glasses or contacts was liberating. Until a few years later, when I developed astigmatism *after* LASIK, so that I again needed corrective lenses.

That surgery was just like the clarity you have when you are so focused on your goals that you avoid being pulled in different directions by distractions. And like that astigmatism, sometimes things might happen to blur your vision again.

Challenges will come up along the way. The best way to not get off track is to remember why you wanted the change in the first place. Stay close to what motivates you, and keep your vision front and center. Your vision might get a little blurry sometimes. That's okay; you can get it corrected.

As you check goals off your list, set new ones. Go back to the SWOT Analysis for your Life Viewpoints and update them based on your new accomplishments. Check up on your vision to make sure that you are still on the right course for you. Adjust your viewpoints, goals, and activities if you feel you are off track and need to take corrective action. That is why I like to review my vision board every year. I treat it like a vision check up to make sure that I am working on what matters.

Give Yourself Permission

As you went through the activities in *The Full-Plate Detox*, you accepted the challenge to do the uncomfortable. You put in the necessary work to make major changes in how you spend your energy. It was probably messy, and you might still be cleaning up after the process. You will feel that it's a bit rough around the edges and not perfect. Please feel free to be perfectly, imperfect.

Take a break when you need to. Give yourself permission to not be perfect. Give yourself permission to make mistakes. Forgive yourself when you do. It doesn't have to be all or nothing.

You are a work in progress. You are still evolving. Just because you are an adult doesn't mean that you have stopped growing.

Know that you can always make necessary changes and adjustments to live the life you want. Know that you are what you allow. Don't demand perfection from yourself. Allow yourself to make mistakes and to then make the necessary adjustments so that this process works for you.

Keep your expectations realistic. Be honest about your abilities and your current situation. It takes time to make changes, especially as you adopt new behaviors.

Give yourself the gift of time. When you're adopting new habits and making changes, it can take you up to sixty-six days to actually form a new habit.[54] You've probably heard that it only takes twenty-one days, but that's just the first part of the process where your brain wakes up and says, "Hey, she's trying to make changes." The remaining forty-plus days are the key time frame in which your brain embeds the habit and automates the routine. Don't give up too soon. The more attention you give a habit (watering the right habits), the more likely it will be that you will reach the sixty-six days! Stick with it.

Trust the process. I will share one of my dirty little secrets. I spent years as an organizing consultant, helping folks create systems and workflows to manage the mountains of paperwork in their offices. I was super glad that I worked at home and they couldn't see my piles of paper because paper has always been my nemesis.

Early in my corporate life, I had to search for proof that a client had given approval on misprinted promotional merchandise. I dug through my stacks of paper for what felt like an eternity as the CEO of our company sat in a chair and watched me rifle through the piles on my desk. I was mortified.

I eventually found the paperwork, but I have never forgotten the embarrassment and stress that came from not being able to put my hands on that document right away. That night, I stayed in my office late and filed everything.

I made it a practice to make sure I knew where the client-approved proofs were. I created a system. I eventually shared that system with others. I fought tooth and nail to win back the respect of the CEO. (Yes, I did.)

I know the importance of creating a system that works for you and sticking to it. That was one of the reasons why I chose organizing and productivity as my field. That situation created a drive in me to always put my best foot forward and help others do the same.

Creating your system was the big win. Now that you have your system, you'll be able to press the reset button when the process goes off track. Just go back through each step again.

Be Kind to Yourself

Don't let Negative Nelly's voice crowd out your growth mindset mantras. Developing an attitude of reflection and gratitude to reflect on your accomplishments will keep that voice quiet. Be conscious of only letting Nelly out when you're wearing your black hat, and put her back in the box when you're done with her.

Take the time to look back with appreciation on what you have accomplished, no matter how small they seem. Remember to celebrate even the little wins in your journey.

Practice mindfulness. Be present and actively engaged in whatever you are doing right now. Being in the moment is about focusing on the experience and using all of your senses to absorb it. Don't look too far down the road, worrying about what is coming. Enjoy what you are doing right now.

When you feel stuck, just do one thing. Start somewhere and then figure out your next step when you get there. Focus on what you can control. If life starts to become hectic again, stop and think about what aspect of your schedule you can control.

I live in a region known for horrendous traffic. I can't do a thing about the traffic except give myself extra travel time, not plan more than a couple of errands at a time, and bring entertainment for my journey. I can't change the traffic, but I can change how I approach it.

Sometimes less is more. The whole point of doing the detox is so that you can enjoy more of what you love. Don't pack your calendar with so much stuff that you jump back on the hamster wheel. Build in down time.

When my clients tell me that they have slipped up on scheduling their priorities, they have usually fallen off the calendaring wagon. They don't want to schedule every minute. I'll tell you what I tell them: You don't have to schedule every minute. Time blocks are really about giving you the flexibility to do what you need to do, when you need to do it. A time block could be dedicated to rest and relaxation. Schedule a break, for goodness sakes!

Okay, that's it!

I hope you have finished this book in a much better place than where you started. Doing the work to get back to the top of your priority list is not selfish. It's you working smarter to keep your energy cup full so you can give from your overflow and still have plenty left over for yourself.

Let's connect. It would be amazing to hear how your connection with your vision has changed your actions and your world. Join me over in the Full-Plate Detox Lounge on Facebook or drop me a line any time by going to FullPlateDetox.com (there are a few additional resources for you there too).

My wish for you is that your plate is full of what you crave and your energy cup is continually refilled.

Thank you for letting me be a part of your full-plate detox.

ENDNOTES

1   Shelby Lorman, "Life Stresses Women Out More Than Men," *Thrive Global*, March 16, 2017, https://thriveglobal.com/stories/life-stresses-women-out-more-than-men/.

2   "The Holmes-Rahe Stress Inventory," *The American Institute of Stress*, accessed October 14, 2019, https://www.stress.org/holmes-rahe-stress-inventory.

3   Ibid.

4   "Women Have More Active Brains Than Men," *Journal of Alzheimer's Disease*, August 7, 2017, https://www.j-alz.com/content/women-have-more-active-brains-men.

5   Ibid.

6   Maricar Santos, *Working Mother*, "When You Factor in Family Duties, the Average Working Mom Works 98 Hours a Week," December 21, 2018, https://www.workingmother.com/when-you-factor-in-family-duties-average-working-mom-works-98-hours-week.

7   Dan Thurmon, *Off Balance on Purpose: Embrace Uncertainty and Create a Life You Love* (Georgia: Motivation Works, 2016).

8   Lizzie Porter, *The Telegraph*, "What happens when a plane loses cabin pressure?" September 21, 2018, https://www.telegraph.co.uk/travel/travel-truths/what-happens-when-a-plane-loses-cabin-pressure/.

9   Shahilla Barok, "Did You Know...You Have Between 50,000 And 70,000 Thoughts Per Day..." *Huffington Post UK*, February 9, 2016, https://www.huffingtonpost.co.uk/shahilla-barok/did-you-knowyou-have-betw_b_11819532.html?guccounter=1&guce_referrer=aHR0cHM6Ly93d3cuZ29vZ2xlLmNvbS8&guce_referrer_sig=AQAAAMJ8Yh8STSjINdaL8fxndBPFrYjann_jv_ihOik

ENDNOTES

ON2BkfW5z8J0VhndIFzQiPynSvkqs_1FEx_AQrwuLwSvCGalY_sqqp_oJ-4HGtXwptLVQ383NU8h95mg746qYOhVAi7UGc4tbt0JO6be8oHo2Wusjj6d0uKs0nD1TQo7-xqxF.

10 Raj Raghunathan PhD, *Psychology Today*, "How Negative is Your 'Mental Chatter'?" October 10, 2013, https://www.psychologytoday.com/us/blog/sapient-nature/201310/how-negative-is-your-mental-chatter.

11 "Watch Your Thoughts, They Become Words; Watch Your Words, They Become Actions," *Quote Investigator*, accessed October 23, 2019, https://quoteinvestigator.com/2013/01/10/watch-your-thoughts/.

12 Steve Harvey, *Act Like a Success, Think Like a Success: Discovering Your Gift and the Way to Life's Riches* (New York: Amistad, 2014).

13 "But They Did Not Give Up," The University of Kentucky, accessed October 23, 2019, https://www.uky.edu/~eushe2/Pajares/OnFailingG.html.

14 Karen Talavera, "Carrot, Egg or Coffee: Which Are You?" *Huffington Post*, November 29, 2011, https://www.huffpost.com/entry/carrot-coffee-egg-parable_b_1107628.

15 The Holmes-Rahe Stress Inventory," https://www.stress.org/holmes-rahe-stress-inventory.

16 Kevin Kruse, "Stephen Covey: 10 Quotes That Can Change Your Life," Forbes, July 16, 2012, https://www.forbes.com/sites/kevinkruse/2012/07/16/the-7-habits/#43dcdac039c6.

17 Ibid.

18 "Pareto Principle," Investopedia, August 29, 2019, https://www.investopedia.com/terms/p/paretoprinciple.asp.

19 Lewis Carroll, *Alice in Wonderland* (New York: Charles E. Merrill Co., 1911).

20 Peter Reuell, "The Power of Picturing Thoughts," *The Harvard Gazette*, May 11, 2017, https://news.harvard.edu/gazette/story/2017/05/visual-images-often-intrude-on-verbal-thinking-study-says/.

21 Lori Ansbach Eckert, "The Effects of Mental Imagery on Free Throw Performance," The College at Brockport: State University of New York, August, 1989, https://digitalcommons.brockport.edu/cgi/viewcontent.cgi?article=1002&context=pes_theses.

22 Joe Greene, *The 48 Laws of Power*, (New York: Penguin Books, 1998, 2000).

23 Barbara Hemphill, accessed October 23, 2019, https://barbarahemphill.com/.

24 A common saying with slight variations attributed to many people.

25 Carole S. Dweck, PhD, *Mindset: The New Psychology of Success*, (New York: Ballantine, 2006, 2016).

26 Heidi Grant Halvorson, PhD, *Succeed: How We Can Reach Our Goals*, (New York: Penguin, 2010).

27 Joel A. Barker, Quoteland.com, accessed October 23, 2019, http://www.quoteland.com/author/Joel-A-Barker-Quotes/2907/.

28 A common saying used in the military and business. The specific attribution is unknown.

29 "Antoine de Saint Exupéry," Wikiquote, updated August 6, 2019, accessed October 23, 2019, https://en.wikiquote.org/wiki/Antoine_de_Saint_Exup%C3%A9ry.

30 "If You Fail To Prepare You Are Preparing To Fail," Quote Investigator.com, accessed October 23, 2019, https://quoteinvestigator.com/2018/07/08/plan/.

31 While this quote has commonly been attributed to Benjamin Franklin, there is no solid evidence that this saying originated with him.

32 "Plans Are Worthless, But Planning Is Everything," Quote Investigator.com, October 23, 2019, https://quoteinvestigator.com/2017/11/18/planning/.

33 While this quote is commonly attributed to Dwight D. Eisenhower, President Eisenhower himself credited an anonymous soldier as the source.

34 "Life is What Happens To You While You're Busy Making Other Plans," Quote Investigator.com, accessed October 23, 2019, https://quoteinvestigator.com/2012/05/06/other-plans/.

35 Edward de Bono, "Six Thinking Hats," The de Bono Group, LLC, accessed October 23, 2019, http://www.debonogroup.com/six_thinking_hats.php.

36 Brian P. Moran, *The 12 Week Year* , (New Jersey: John Wiley & Sons, Inc., 2013).

37 Malcolm D. Lee, dir., *Girls Trip (2017)*. 2017; Universal Pictures.

38 Gyeorgos C. Hatonn, *The Mother of All Webs Who Gotcha!* (America West Publishers, 1992), 99.

39 Carl Sandberg, "Carl Sandberg Quotes," Brainy Quote.com, accessed October 23, 2019, https://www.brainyquote.com/quotes/carl_sandburg_121791.

ENDNOTES

40 Carl Duhigg, *The Power of Habit: Why We Do What We Do in Life and Business* (New York: Random House, 2012).

41 The quote has previously been attributed to Mark Twain, but the correct author is Nicholas Chamfort.

42 "Eat a Live Frog Every Morning, and Nothing Worse Will Happen to You the Rest of the Day," Quote Investigator.com, accessed October 23, 2019, https://quoteinvestigator.com/2013/04/03/eat-frog/.

43 Brian Tracy, *Eat That Frog!: 21 Great Ways to Stop Procrastinating and Get More Done in Less Time* (Oakland: Brett-Koehler Publishers, 2017).

44 "Bruce Lee Quotes," Brainy Quote.com, accessed October 23, 2019, https://www.brainyquote.com/quotes/bruce_lee_384548.

45 "Joel A. Barker," http://www.quoteland.com/author/Joel-A-Barker-Quotes/2907/.

46 "Walt Disney Quotes," Brainy Quote.com, Accessed October 23, 2019, https://www.brainyquote.com/quotes/walt_disney_130027.

47 Pass It On.com, accessed October 23, 2019, https://www.passiton.com/inspirational-quotes/7524-a-river-cuts-through-rock-not-because-of-its.

48 "Procrastination is the thief of time," Encyclopedia.com, accessed October 23, 2019, https://www.encyclopedia.com/humanities/dictionaries-thesauruses-pictures-and-press-releases/procrastination-thief-time.

49 "Pele Quotes," Brainy Quote.com, accessed October 23, 2019, https://www.brainyquote.com/quotes/pele_737774.

50 "Henry Ford quotes," Brainy Quote.com, accessed October 23, 2019, https://www.brainyquote.com/quotes/henry_ford_121339.

51 "It Always Seems Impossible Until It's Done," Quote Investigator.com, accessed October 23, 2019, https://quoteinvestigator.com/2016/01/05/done/.

52 "But They Did Not Give Up," https://www.uky.edu/~eushe2/Pajares/OnFailingG.html.

53 Robert Stevenson, dir., *Mary Poppins*, 1964, Walt Disney Studios, Burbank.

54 John M. Grohol, PysD, "Need to Form a New Habit? Give Yourself At Least 66 Days," Psych Central.com, accessed October 23, 2019, https://psychcentral.com/blog/need-to-form-a-new-habit-66-days/.

ACKNOWLEDGMENTS

With incredible gratitude and appreciation, I'd like to thank and acknowledge:

My family of SHEros—my mommy Noblin; sisters Llona and Suzanne; and my niece Eliana—strong women who "tek likkle and mek much".

Eileen, Maureen, Ruth, Natasha, and Nadia—you've been there since the very beginning!

The original Visionary Goal Getters- Angela, Erica, Pam, Tanisha, and Janelle. Thank you for holding me accountable, giving me your insights, and cheering me on along the way.

My biz besties and Diva—Heather, Dawn, Janice, and Atheneé who have believed in me through my biz journey. Thank you for the truth telling and never-ending support. You ladies rock!

My mentors PJ, Liz, Barbara, Andrea, Kathy and Sandra- thank you for leading with strength.

My book coach and publisher, Teresa, for holding my hand, keeping me focused, and making me stretch my comfort zone.

ACKNOWLEDGMENTS

My clients who trusted the process, worked through their challenges, and allowed me to guide them through their seasons of significant growth.

ALL the everyday super SHEros in my life: The incredible women who lead their families, businesses, teams, ministries, and communities with smiles on their faces, a can-do attitude, and hearts full of love.

My Lord and Savior Jesus Christ. I know I can do all things through You. You are my strength, guiding light, and never-failing counselor.

ABOUT THE AUTHOR

Nicole Chamblin, MA, CTPC®, CPBA®, RCC® is **a Chief Visionary and Productivity Coach who loves helping busy women get back to the top of their priority list.** She is a "procrastination-proof" coach and trainer who delivers powerful, yet loving kicks in the behind to frustrated, exhausted women who have been running on the hamster wheel for far too long.

Nicole loves helping busy SHEros connect with their vision, communicate their goals, and collaborate more productively. When they work with her, they learn to kick self-defeating behaviors, knock out their task lists, and fill their empty cups—guilt free!

Dedicated to translating knowledge into action, Nicole shares practical strategies to take her clients from busy and overwhelmed, to productive and giving from their overflow!

Nicole loves sharing nuggets of wisdom through training, coaching, and mentoring programs. Hundreds of busy professionals in private sector, local, and federal government agencies have benefited from her practical down-to-earth approach to the productivity challenges we all face every day.

Through her signature program the Full Plate Detox, she inspires SHEros to connect with their vision, lock in their goals, and create success plans to live their dreams.

Nicole believes in walking her talk, collaborating with like minded visionaries, and sharing her gifts to help others shine. An island girl transplanted to the cold streets of NYC, she now lives in Northern Virginia with her husband and son.